The Secrets We Keep

TICH BREWSTER

The Secrets We Keep

Tich Brewster

Copyright © 2024 Tich Brewster

Cover design by Coffin Print Designs

Interior design by Vanilla Lily Designs

Editing/Proofreading by Lea Vickery

This is a work of fiction.

All names, characters, places, and events are the work of the author's imagination. Any resemblance to real person, places, or events is coincidental.

The Secrets We Keep

ISBN 979-8-218-54945-9 (softcover)

Release date December 13th, 2024

All rights reserved. No part of this book may be reproduced or transmitted in any form or by any means, electronic or mechanical, including photocopying and recording, without permission in writing from the author or publisher.

Scanning, uploading, and distribution of this book via the Internet, or by any other means, without permission from author or publisher are illegal and punishable by law.

Published by Twisty Plots

Acknowledgements

I want to thank all my readers for the continued support. You guys are awesome and mean the world to me. Big hugs and kisses to you all.

A big thank you to Teresa and Shalisha for standing by my side on this crazy journey. You two have supported me from the beginning. Love you girls to the moon and back.

Christina and Kris are my rockstars. Those two do so much for me behind the scenes that allow me to spend more time behind the screen typing the words for your reading pleasure. Thank you, girls, for taking good care of me. XOXO

ONE
Monika

Today is a big day here at the veterinary clinic. For the past week, we have been preparing for our new veterinarian. Some hotshot doctor from the city is coming in to take over for our retiring doctor. He's supposed to be the best in the state, and one who expects perfection from his staff. In other words, he's a hard ass. Which is great, don't get me wrong, but I'm so new in this business, what happens if I make too many mistakes for his liking. Will he fire me for asking too many questions?

Gah, get a grip, Monika.

I can feel my blood pressure rise just thinking about it. This is what happens when you're an overthinker. You question everything you say and do, including everything you've yet to say and do. All the other assistants and technicians are going about their day with business-as-usual attitudes, and I'm over here about to have a coronary. Instead of being able to focus on work, I'm stressing over all the possible ways I could screw up in front of the new boss and get myself fired.

Speaking of fired, if that were to happen, what the hell would I do? This town is so small, we have a couple of gas stations and that's it. If we want to eat out or go grocery shopping, we travel to the next town over. Don't get me wrong, I could—and would if necessary—work at one of our gas stations, or drive the ten minutes to work at the SuperMarket or fast food, but the income

I would make from those places wouldn't compare to what I'm making now.

On top of all of this, I'm supposed to have dinner with my best friend, Amy, and her brother tonight. Silas is my childhood crush. The one guy I would sit around fantasizing about. I had hidden notebooks with his name scribbled inside. As a kid, he was the one guy I dreamed about marrying. I wanted the white picket fence and everything.

Did I ever tell Amy about my crush on her brother? Hell to the no. Why, you ask. One, that girl wanted me far away from her dweeb—her words, not mine— of a brother. The two of them did not get along, he couldn't be bothered by two bratty kids such as us. The second reason, he was four grades ahead of us. Far too old to notice a child like me, but I sure as hell noticed him.

Jeez, just thinking about Silas is stirring up those old feelings that I thought I had buried long ago.

Hmm, I wonder if he is still the tall athletic type. Silas played soccer in school and had a tall, lean body with thick calves that flexed with every step. I bet he is still as gorgeous as ever. Guess I'll find out tonight. Hopefully he hasn't forgotten about me. Who am I kidding? Silas only knew me as the annoying kid that came over to play with his baby sister. The man probably doesn't even remember that Amy had any close friends, let alone me.

Approaching footsteps draw me out of my thoughts. "Monika?" Doctor Allen smiles as he enters the back room, where I'm currently watching over a kitten that has come out of surgery.

Running my finger over the kitten's tiny little toes, I stand from the stool. "Yes, Doctor Allen?" Doctor Allen has been nothing but kind to me since I started working here. He is kind of like an extra grandfather and I'm sad to see him go. Hopefully he will come by to visit from time-to-time.

"Doctor McKade just arrived." He gestures for me to follow him. "Come say hello."

Doctor McKade. Even his name gives off the hard ass vibe. As I follow Doctor Allen out of the back room, I get stuck on the name McKade. Somewhere in the recesses of my mind, it rings a bell, but I can't place a finger on it to save my life.

The name is not a common name around here, but still vaguely familiar. Maybe a name I've heard on a television show, or one I've read in a book? Who the hell knows? Mentally shrugging my shoulders, I continue down the long corridor to meet our new veterinarian.

What I notice first is that the new doctor is not in scrubs like our current doctor. The new guy is wearing a suit with those expensive shiny black shoes. But that's not what gives me pause. No, what causes my steps to falter are those familiar gray eyes. Now the name McKade rings loud and clear. Doctor McKade is Amy's older brother. Silas McKade.

Silas and Amy have different fathers, so their last names are not the same. As a kid, I think I only heard his last name a time or two. Which is why it didn't click when Doctor Allen spoke of Doctor McKade.

What I want to know is why Amy didn't tell me her brother went to school to become a veterinarian. Of course, she doesn't really talk much about him at all. After he left for college, he didn't come back around, except for the holidays. So, there has been zero chances for me to get to know him. Until now, apparently.

When Jose, one of the assistants, clears his throat, I continue my trek across the room. Silas doesn't smile or give any indication that he recognizes me. In fact, his expression is void of any emotion at all. Those beautiful gray eyes that have haunted my dreams since childhood are cold and distanced. I don't know whether to smile and extend my hand in greeting, or fade into the background.

Fading into the background is thrown out the door when Doctor Allen smiles warmly at me, swinging his hand in my direction. "This is Monika. She is one of our technicians."

"Nice to meet you." Silas's words are monotone, and he doesn't give me a second glace before turning his attention back to the paperwork in his hand. Talk about cold. The man doesn't exude any type of friendly vibes at all. Sheesh, I sure hope he has better manners when it comes to the customers and pets.

Like a fool, I stand here waiting. Waiting for what, I don't know. I mean, surely, he doesn't greet his staff this poorly. Or is it just me that he is greeting this way? Flipping through the pages in his hand, Silas walks around the desk, taking a seat on the other side.

Striking up conversation with Doctor Allen, he completely dismisses the rest of us standing in his office. This behavior is so odd and nothing like the Silas I once knew. The Silas I remember was funny and kind. Always including everyone into conversation and inviting them on outings.

Everyone but his baby sister and her best friend, that is.

Now, as I stare at the man that I once had a major childhood crush on, he is nothing more than a stuck-up asshole. Definitely not the same kind-hearted soul that lived in my fantasies. Who am I kidding, he still lives in my dreams.

"Come on." Jose gently grips my elbow and leads me from the room.

As I step over the threshold, I glance back at Silas. With his head bent over those blasted papers, he continues talking with Doctor Allen. For no reason at all, my heart shatters. I know my heartache is uncalled for since we never had any kind of relationship, but all the admiring I did from a distance as a child and all the fantasizing, my heart breaks with his lack of recognition.

God, does that make me pathetic?

"Hey, what's up with you?" Jose asks, lifting his eyebrow as he looks me over.

What am I supposed to say? *Oh, well, my lovesick ass is mourning something it never had to begin with.* Absolutely not, he would think I've lost my ever-loving mind. "What do you mean?"

"Uh, uh." Stopping in his tracks, he spins me around. "We're not playing this game."

"What game?" I really wish he would just drop this, but my friend knows me too well.

"The game where you play dumb in an attempt to ditch the conversation." Brown pools stare intently as he awaits an explanation. Damn him for always knowing how to get me to confess all my secrets.

"It's nothing." Glancing around, I make sure no one is in earshot before I divulge any information. "I, um." Lowering my voice to a whisper, I say, "I know Silas." Squeezing my eyes shut, I correct myself. "I mean, I know Doctor McKade."

A smile curves Jose's mouth. "Is he an ex?" Tugging me further down the hall, he quietly shuts the door to the empty lounge as we enter. "That's it isn't it? I saw the way you froze when you laid eyes on him."

"No," I hiss, not wanting anyone to catch wind of this. "He is not my ex. Silas is my best friend's older brother."

Jose is quiet for a few moments, and I can see the wheels in his head turning, trying to figure out this situation. "I assume we're talking about Amy's older brother?" he questions. When I nod to confirm, he leans a hip against the wall. "You mean to tell me that Silas is Amy's brother? Isn't her last name Baker?"

Rolling my eyes is not what I mean to do, but they sort of have a mind of their own. "Yes." His brows furrow as he mulls over my answer, so I decide to give him an explanation for their differing names. "They have different fathers."

Understanding dawns and he nods his head. "Oh, that makes sense." Jose and I are close, almost as close as Amy and me, yet I've never spoken to him about Silas. Never felt the need to reveal to another soul that at the age of fourteen I became obsessed with a guy who was eighteen. Point two seconds later his eyes widen, like a lightbulb being switched on. "If he's not an ex, does this mean he's a secret crush?"

"Shh." I wave my hands wildly in the air. "Keep your voice down." The last thing I need is for this tidbit of information to get back to Silas. I can only imagine what he would think of me, let alone how this would affect our working relationship. Heat creeps into my cheeks and I know he can see my embarrassment when he smirks.

"So, I'm right?" Does he have to keep on the subject? Aren't guys put off by gossip? One would think Jose would just let this go, not dig deep into my secrets, but here he is acting like a middle school girl gossiping about the latest news. "How long has the obsession been going on?"

"Look, it's just some dumb teenage crush. I'm totally over it." My words are a complete rush as I speak. Also, a complete lie. "It was years and years ago. Let's just get back to work and never speak of this again."

Opening the lounge door, I step into the hallway and speed walk back toward the recovery room when I see Silas walking this way. No way in hell I want to be in his vicinity right now. So, I keep my head down and rush past.

My only mission is to get through this day.

TWO
Silas

The moment she stepped foot into the office I knew who she was. Only now she is all grown up. Monika moved in next door to us my Senior year of high school. She was four years younger than me, but that didn't keep me from noticing her. Sure, at first, she was just my little sister's annoying friend, but one day I noticed a couple of boys tormenting her. Not the *I've got a crush on you* kind of tormenting either. No, these punks were bullying her because she wasn't the typical stick thin girl with straight hair you see in magazines.

When I saw them throwing rocks at her and taunting her, I saw red. Never in my life had I felt the need to smash someone's face in, but seeing that, yeah, that's how I felt. I stepped out of the house like my ass was on fire, yelling and threatening to beat up these little punks. Not that I would have actually touched them, they were just kids and I had just turned eighteen, a legal adult, but I did scare them shitless.

Once those stupid kids ran off, I took notice of her scraped knees and hands. My guess is they pushed her down. All because she didn't fit the mold. Sure, she had more curves than most of the girls at school, but there was nothing wrong with those curves.

That day I vowed to be the protector she needed. No, I didn't hang around her and my sister, there was too much of an age gap for that. Besides, who in their right mind wants to listen to a couple of fourteen-year-old girls gossip about guys and whatever else they chat about. What I did, was make sure all the kids knew that if they messed with Monika, they'd have to deal with me.

Now, here we are ten years later, and this girl is full blown woman. In every way. My mouth went dry when I looked up and seen her standing there. Immediately, my eyes went to her ring finger, needing to know if she was taken. Because, damn, who wouldn't want a woman like her by their side?

But like ice water to the face, I remembered she's still my sister's best friend. Not only that, but now she is my employee, which is another type of off-limits. The only thing I could think to do to keep myself from acting like a fool and kissing her in front of everyone was to shut down all my emotions.

I noticed it immediately. The effect my indifference made, but it was necessary in order to keep my body in check. And let me tell you, a certain part of my body took notice right away and the last thing I want is for my staff to see me sporting a boner in the middle of work. No one would take me seriously if they witnessed that. So, here I am, sitting behind the desk, pretending to listen to every word coming out of Doctor Allen's mouth. When in reality, my thoughts are with the one woman that is one hundred percent off limits.

The majority of my day is spent going over the books and current patient files. Thankfully there are no surgeries scheduled for today. Doctor Allen attends to the few pets that are brought in for check-ups. This allows me to get a few things in order, while also giving him one last day taking care of the animals he has grown to love.

One-by-one, the staff exits the facility as their jobs are done for the day. A glance at my watch lets me know that I am running low on time. I need to get home and shower if I intend to make it to the restaurant on time. The last thing I want to do is show up late for our dinner, especially since I haven't seen my sister in the last six months.

Locking my office door, I trek through the building, making

sure everything is clean and the computers are shut down. As I round the corner to check the backdoor, I run smack into a body. A warm, lush body. The scream that echoes down the corridor pierces my eardrums, and as I glance up at her, she is clutching her chest.

Wide blue eyes peer up at me. "Oh my god, Silas, I thought I was alone." As if she just realized her mistake, she backtracks. "I'm sorry, I meant to say, Doctor McKade."

I lift a brow but otherwise make no move to acknowledge her slipup. "It's getting late, why don't you head out and I'll finish locking up."

Cocking her head to the side, she opens her mouth like she has something to say but closes it instead. It would probably be the polite thing for me to ask if she needs anything, or if there is something that I could help her with, but rather than striking up conversation, I dowse the situation in cold water by stepping around her and continuing to the backdoor.

A huff leaves her pretty lips as soon as I'm out of view. There is a smile that curves mine, knowing that I get under her skin. Speaking of getting under her skin. I'd like to get under her in a whole different manner. Just thinking about it has my pants growing tighter against my groin.

Driving across town takes all of five minutes. This town takes the word small-town to a whole new meaning. Morris has an elementary school, middle/high school, a post office, a couple gas stations, and a dollar store. The dollar store is new, we didn't have one of those when I lived here before.

Crossing the threshold, I toss my keys and wallet on the table and head straight for the shower. Dinner with my sister is the last thing I feel like doing tonight, but it's not an event I would blow off either. We haven't seen enough of each other over the last ten years. It's time to rectify that.

Since I'm low on time, I speed wash and change into a fitted black tee and a pair of faded blue jeans. As I'm tying my shoes, my text alert goes off. One guess who it might be. Standing from my bed, I pick up my cell phone from the dresser. I was correct in my guessing. It's my sister.

> Amy: Hey, bum. I'm here.

Of course, she is. My sister always has to outdo me.

> Silas: You're a brat. We agreed to dinner at seven. You're twenty minutes early.

> Amy: And as usual, you're pushing it. Always waiting until the last minute.

My eyes roll of their own accord.

> Silas: I do not wait until the last minute. I'm a doctor with a busy schedule.

> Amy: Yeah, yeah, whatever. Just hurry.

Shoving my wallet in one pocket and my cell phone in the other, I head out of the house and to my car. The drive to the restaurant in the next town over only takes fifteen minutes. Parking next to her silver Camry, I shoot her a text to let her know I'm here.

> Silas: Walking in.

> Amy: About time. We're in the back room to the far left.

We? Did she bring a boyfriend with her? Shuffling through the crowd, I make my way to the back room. Scanning the sea of faces, I finally lay eyes on my sister. The person sitting beside her is not who I expected to see. Amy is talking, using her hands as she has a habit of doing, and Monika laughs. Her whole face lights up as she does.

My steps faulter because of the beauty that radiates from

Monika. As kids, I always thought she was pretty, but now. Now she is so much more. Amy spots me first and waves her arms in the air like she's trying to direct a plane to the runway. I swear my sister has no subtle bone in her body.

Monika follows Amy's gaze, and the smile drops from her face, that sparkle in her eye diming as she zeros in on me. Apparently, I am continuing with the prick-like facade as I remember our working status. It's just easier this way. My gaze shifts from hers and goes back to my sister. Only then do I smile and greet her with a hug, completely ignoring Monika.

Oblivious to the shift in her best friend's mood, Amy gestures toward Monika. "Silas, you remember Monika. My BFF that lived next door to us when we were kids?"

"She did?" Glancing over at Monika, I say, "I don't remember." Of course, I remember. The sadness that flashes in her blue pools is brief, but I see it, and I hate myself for making her feel insignificant. "But we did meet today at the clinic."

"That's right." Monika shifts uncomfortably in her seat, not meeting my gaze.

"I'm so glad you two are working together." Amy is beaming as she takes my hand in her right and Monika's hand in her left.

The second she lets go of my hand, I stand up and suggest we get our plates. The one decent restaurant in Okmulgee is a buffet. Not that I'm complaining. Buffets are perfect for me as I can eat my weight in food and then some.

By the time I am done making my rounds at the three buffet lines, I'm carrying two plates of food, a plate piled high with salad, and a dessert plate all strategically placed on a tray. Monika's eyebrows shoot up to her hairline when she sees what I have in my hands. I smirk at her shock, clearly, she isn't used to men with such an appetite.

As we eat, Amy carries most of the conversation. That girl can talk your ear off about everything under the sun. How are we even related? Finishing my first plate of food, I move on to my salad when I notice that Monika is still eating, or rather picking at her first plate that only had a small amount of salad on it to begin with.

I seem to remember that she loved barbeque chicken as a kid, so I stab a thigh with my fork and offer it to her. Her lips form a tight smile, and she shakes her head. Lifting a brow, I slide the piece of chicken back onto my plate and scoot it toward her. "Help yourself."

Shaking her head, she moves salad around her plate with a fork. I get the feeling she would rather be anywhere other than here, sitting across from me.

Setting my fork down, I scoot my chair back. "Would you like me to get you something else from the buffet?"

Preparing to stand, I'm not expecting what she says next. "No thanks, I'm not really hungry tonight."

Not hungry? Unless she went home and ate before coming to the restaurant with my sister, she hasn't eaten more than half a banana today. I know because like a stalker, I watched her eat lunch with the others today. Half a banana and a glass of water was all that touched her lips.

Nobody can resist chocolate cake, so I point at the dessert plate. "How about cake, everyone loves a good chocolate cake?"

Those blue pools slide over to the piece of cake on my plate, and they brighten. I'm already scooting the plate toward her when she shakes her head. Again. "Thanks, but I'm good."

It's unsettling watching her pick at her salad. A salad that only consists of greens, onions, and a vinaigrette. Why didn't she add meat, veggies, olives, the whole shebang? Maybe she's coming down with a cold and doesn't have much of an appetite. Who knows?

Well, at least I tried.

Deciding to leave it at that, I dig into my meal while keeping an eye on her lack of eating. Surely, it's a stomach issue and not just because I'm sitting at the table. Right? I'll have to keep an eye on her. If she's ill, she'll need to cash in sick days so she can recover.

THREE
Monika

The next day, I show up for work over an hour early because we have back-to-back surgeries all morning and I want to get things ready. When I spot the black Audi in the parking lot, dread fills me. I'm not sure I can handle Silas's cold demeanor this early in the morning. Especially since I have yet to have my cup of coffee.

Mentally tugging up my big girl panties, I shut off the car and head inside. As I walk past his office, Silas glances up. "Hey."

Taking a step back, I poke my head in the doorway. I didn't expect him to be friendly, especially after his rude behavior yesterday. This is a welcome surprise. "Hey." I'm not sure what else to say. Yeah, he was polite enough last night, but that was because his sister was sitting across from him and who would want to show their stony and dismissive side in the presence of their family?

Pointing toward the coffee mug on the desk next to his computer, he turns his attention back to the screen. "Bring me another cup, would you?"

No, *good morning*, just, *bring me another cup, would you?* If this is how our day will pan out, I'm going to need more than one cup of coffee this morning. I may need a whole pot to deal with this man. "Sure."

Stomping across the room, I snatch his mug off the desk and stomp right back out. I don't care that I'm acting childish. His damn attitude is childish. Seriously, is it really so hard to be sociable? Jeez.

When I enter the lounge, I sigh in relief to see a full pot of coffee. That means I don't have to mess with, or wait for, the coffee maker to brew before pouring my own cup. Opening the cabinet, I grab my black coffee mug with the phrase *Coffee before Talkie*. This saying is particularly true this morning.

After pouring my cup, I refill Mr. Unapproachable's cup. This time when I enter, he doesn't even bother lifting his head. Since I didn't sleep well last night, I'm extra grouchy. And because I'm butthurt that he didn't remember me, I decide to act out. Juvenile? Yeah. Do I care? Nope, not even a little. With a wicked smirk on my face, I set his mug on the far corner of his desk, just out of reach.

I may regret doing that later after I've had plenty of caffeine, but for the time being, score one for Monika. My cup is completely empty by the time I make it back to the lounge and I swear it's like I didn't consume any at all. My brain is still half asleep.

Two cups later, I'm in the operating room, getting things in order. Today's surgeries include four sterilizations and a tumor removal on a Pitbull. The latter will require overnight staff to ensure he recovers okay.

As I finish setting up the tray for our first patient, I hear Jose's bright and cheery voice down the hall. "Good morning, everybody." With him here, the work environment is bound to be better than it is currently. At least he's friendly. When I make my way back to the lounge, Jose is pouring coffee in my abandoned cup. God bless his soul.

"Thanks." I sip my fourth cup of java as I watch him peel open a Snickers bar. Oh, how I wish I could eat chocolate for breakfast. Unfortunately, I was not gifted with the skinny gene. My previous boyfriend made a point to remind me of that fact every day we were together.

Jose is oblivious to my inner turmoil as he munches on his sugary goodness. Only one person knows of the verbal abuse I suffered for the past few years. Amy. I would be mortified if anyone else caught wind of the things that man said to me. Hell, I would be mortified if Amy knew the extent of the abuse I endured. I've never divulged the true hell I underwent at the hands of my ex.

Thank God that monster found another woman to obsess over. Now, I don't have to listen to his degrading words day in and day out. Or suffer by his hand on his bad days. I just hope that he isn't treating his new girl the same as he did me.

Volunteers start filing in which means it's time to get this workday started. As if reading my mind, Silas pauses in the doorway, snapping his fingers. "Come on, tech, it's time to get this show on the road."

Tech?

Can he not be bothered to remember my name? It was one thing when he had no recollection of me yesterday but come on. You mean to tell me the man can't take the time to memorize the names of his staff? Unbelievable.

Raising a brow, he asks, "Don't you like your job, tech?"

The question throws me off and I'm not sure what he's asking me at first. "Yes, of course I do."

"Then learn to manage your time properly and be punctual." With those parting words, Silas is off to the operating room.

Manage my time and be punctual? Did he miss the part where I came in early to prep for today? I hope that dumbass stubs his toe or sits on a thumbtack. How dare he suggest I'm not punctual.

Jose's mouth opens and closes like a fish chasing food pellets. Apparently, he is as shocked as I am hearing those words. "Damn, I heard he was a hard ass, but that was downright rude."

"You got that right." Well, this morning just went from bad to worse.

The surgeries went well, and all our patients are currently resting comfortably in their kennels. Two of the volunteers are on watch duty while Jose goes for his lunch break. When we have patients in recovery, either Jose or I are present at all times. This allows for quick care in the event of an emergency.

My phone buzzes with an incoming message.

> Amy: Drinks tonight?

I wish.

> Monika: Not tonight, I'm working overnight.

Which is going to suck, by the way, because I'm running on fumes already and it's not even one o'clock. Yes, Jose is splitting this time with me, but it will still suck staying late. I'll have to make a run to the gas station for a couple energy drinks before we close.

Time passes faster than I realize. In no time, Jose is tapping my shoulder to relieve me of my duties, allowing me to leave for my break. Thank God, maybe I will be able to catch a couple minutes of shuteye.

Relief washes over me when I see that the lounge is empty. This means I don't have to pretend that I'm not hungry to prevent my co-workers from questioning me on my lack of food. Or avoid looking at them so they don't see the longing on my face when they bite into their flavorful meals.

For once I want to bite into a juicy cheeseburger without hearing Brandon's voice in my head telling me I'm too fat and unattractive. If he didn't like the way I looked, why the hell did he go out with me? Why date me for five years—four of which he lived with me—if he thought I was fat and ugly?

Retrieving my lunch bag from the fridge, I open my container of blueberries and pick at them. Unaware that I'm being watched,

I startle when Silas speaks. "Not hungry?" He points to my measly portion of berries.

How long has he been standing there? I hate when guys question me about my food or appetite. It usually feels like they're judging me the same way Brandon did. Does Silas think I'm fat? Now I'm self-conscious about how I look in my scrubs.

To divert the conversation away from food, I ask him about his time in the city. "How was it, living in the city?"

Raising a brow, he glances back at my tiny container of berries. I can tell he wants to say something more about my choice of food, or whatever. Instead, I'm thoroughly surprised when he drops the subject and answers my question. "It was nice. Traffic is horrific, but they have dozens of museums and other fun activities."

I've been to Oklahoma City exactly two times. Both occasions were back when I was a kid, my parents took me to the amusement park out there. "Sounds exciting, and a bit scary, I hate traffic."

Crossing the room to fetch a Pepsi out of the fridge, he chuckles. "I'm not sure I'd call it scary. A pain in the ass maybe, but not scary." Lifting a can, he asks, "Want one?"

Do I want one? Absolutely I do. I have not had a Pepsi in so long. Just looking at it makes my mouth water. Surely it wouldn't hurt if I had just one. Oh, who am I kidding. If I had one, I wouldn't be able to stop there. I would drink one a day, then two, and before I know it, I would be drinking four a day. "No thanks, I'm good with my water."

Glancing at my large tumbler, he nods and shuts the fridge.

FOUR
Silas

At the end of the day, everyone leaves except for Monika. She stays behind because she is on first watch tonight. Since she doesn't get a break in her shift, I decide to stay behind and tag team the next several hours. That way she can eat a decent dinner and catch an hour or so of sleep. There is no way I would expect anyone to work a straight eighteen hours shift.

Opening the door, I poke my head in and find her sitting in a chair holding the dog's paw. She's softly singing while offering him comfort. I've worked with many technicians over the years that did not show this level of compassion toward the furry patients. Monika is different. The way she loves the animals speaks volumes about her character.

"Hey." I knock on the doorframe. She jolts, twisting in the chair to look at me. "Sorry, didn't mean to scare you. I'm grabbing dinner at the Mexican restaurant. Do you want anything?"

I don't miss the longing in her eyes or the way she licks her lips, like she's savoring the sweetest treat. Sucking her bottom lip between her teeth, she bites the plump flesh as she thinks. Her stomach growls, the sound bouncing off the walls. It must embarrass her because she buries her face in her hands and shakes her head. "I can't believe that just happened."

"Don't worry about it. Mine has been doing the same for the last ten minutes." It hasn't, I keep plenty of snacks on hand because I love food and am constantly eating something. Still, I don't want her to feel embarrassed. Her stomach growling is a very natural response to the body's need for sustenance.

"Yeah, but did your stomach sound like it was trying to eat you from the inside out?" Lifting her tumbler to her lips, she takes a healthy swig while pressing a hand to her stomach.

What I want to say is, *if you had eaten a proper lunch, it wouldn't be so vocal*. Instead, I go a gentler route. "It didn't sound as bad as you think it did." Glancing down at my watch, I nudge her for an answer. "So, what would you like for dinner?"

"You don't need to get me anything. I'm fine but thank you for the offer." Why does it seem like Monika purposely eats light? Not just light, but almost nonexistent.

"It's on me. Think of it as a thank you for working late." That's not a lie, but not entirely the truth either. Yes, I'm buying her dinner for working late, as I would for anyone else. But the real reason behind my offer is because I've witnessed her barely eating on two different occasions. Honestly, it bothers me.

"Fine. I'll take a street taco with chicken. No rice or beans, please." Then she turns her attention back to the Pitbull.

I want to question her but think better of it. Perhaps she has a medical condition and has a low appetite. There's a slew of reasons as to why she eats so little. No matter the reason, I'll keep my mouth shut so she doesn't get offended or embarrassed. For now. On my way out the door, I place a call to the restaurant with our order.

When I get back to the clinic, Monika is trekking toward the lounge. At the sound of my footsteps, she glances up. "Oh, you're back. I was just getting a refill." She waves her tumbler at me as if she needs to verify her words.

"How's Butch?" Butch being the Pitbull.

"He's doing great." She proceeds to tell me about his recovery since I've spent most of my time in the office since the surgery.

"Good, come take a break and eat. Butch will be fine for a few." Carrying the bag to the counter, I set up the spread. Yes, I bought more food than necessary, but I wanted to make sure she had enough to eat without making her feel awkward.

Eyes wide, she takes the paper plate I offer. "I only asked for a taco."

"Tacos are in that box." I point to the one at the far right of the lineup. She grabs her solo taco and sits at the table, watching as I pile my plate with two enchiladas, rice, beans, a tamale, and a taco. On my way to join her, I grab the container of guacamole.

Tracking my every move, she waves her hands when I spoon the green creamy substance onto her plate. "What are you doing? I don't want that."

"You." I lift a brow. "Not wanting guacamole?" Leaving the heap on her plate, I scoop some onto my enchiladas and taco. "Since when do you not want guac?"

"Since—" Stopping short, she narrows those beautiful blue eyes at me. "Excuse me, what did you just say?" Rather than answer, I fork enchilada into my mouth. Aiming a finger at me, she calls me out on my slipup. "You do remember me. You little liar."

I remember more than I should considering our age difference. She may think I didn't see her spying on me from around the corner, or admiring me from across the yard years ago, but I noticed. "Guilty. Now eat."

Using the spoon that I discarded, she adds the tiniest dollop of guacamole to her taco. We eat in comfortable silence. Monika picks at her taco like she's afraid it will grow arms and punch her in the face. Every now and then her stomach continues to rumble and I'm getting a sneaky suspicion that she is purposely not eating.

Memories plague my mind of all the times the kids in the neighborhood would pick on her because of her weight. Monika was never fat, but she wasn't as thin as most of the other girls her age either. Is she restraining herself because she thinks she's overweight?

When she thinks I'm not paying attention, she gazes at my

plate and her stomach growls in response. Without giving it much thought, I cut a piece of my chicken enchilada, scoop a healthy amount of guacamole on top, then hold the fork to her lips.

Jerking back like I've just bitten her; she immediately starts to shake her head. "No, I can't eat that."

"Why?" Examining the food on the fork, I confirm that there is nothing on there she doesn't like. In fact, I made sure to get the foods I remember her enjoying. "The only difference between my enchilada and your taco is the sauce and the way it was cooked."

"Yes, but—" She looks away, seemingly trying to find the words to explain why she can't eat what I've presented. "I just can't."

"Are you allergic to the sauce?"

"No, I'm not allergic." Those blue orbs peer up at me. "They have the best sauce in town."

Wanting to get to the bottom of this, I ask, "Are you diabetic, or have some other medical condition?"

"What?" She looks appalled that I would ask such a question. "No, I don't have a medical condition."

"Good, then there is no reason for you not to take a bite." Holding it back to her lips, I urge her to eat. It's clear that she wants some, her eyes have continuously envied my plate since we sat down to eat.

"There's too many calories." There it is. The culprit, as I suspected, is her weight. Does she not see herself in the mirror? No, she's not stick thin like all the women in the magazines. Not all men are attracted to those types. Most men want a woman with curves. She has curves. Curves in all the right places.

"Forget the calories, it's just one bite." I dated a girl a couple years ago that counted calories and was obsessed with her weight. Drove me crazy.

"But—"

Lifting a brow, I dare her to disobey. "Eat."

Moisture builds in her eyes, and she tilts her head back, batting her eyelids to keep the tears from falling. Did the taunting she endured during childhood affect her this deeply? How badly did the kids tease her after I left?

To my satisfaction, she opens her mouth. A moan slips free as she chews. I'm not entirely sure she's aware she made the noise, because she is gripping the edge of the table and seems blissfully unaware of everything but the food in her mouth.

How is a woman so beautiful, even with a mouth full of food? I could kiss her. In fact, I desperately want to kiss her, and do many dirty things to that body of hers. But as I take in her body, the site of the clinic's name on her scrubs brings me back to reality. In no way, shape, or form can I pursue her.

Turning my attention back to the food in front of me, I fork a piece of tamale. When my mouth closes over the metal, I get a jolt in the pit of my stomach at the thought of my mouth touching where her lips have been.

Again, I'm left imagining kissing her. Would her lips be as soft as they look? I envision pinning her body beneath mine, gripping her thigh tightly as I have my way with her. The moan I heard from her earlier, would she make that same sound as I fill her?

Great, now my mind is in the gutter, and I'm stuck in the clinic *alone* with her. Not a good combination. How am I supposed to survive this night without kissing her senseless? I'll have to lock myself in my office to fight the urge.

Lucky for me, Monika finishes what's left of her taco and stands. "Thank you for dinner. I'm going to sit with Butch." The smile that graces her lips is pure. Angelic. And not at all helping me suppress the lust I feel when around her.

I nod but otherwise don't look at her. If I'm going to keep my hands to myself when in her presence, then I'm going to have to turn back into asshole Silas.

FIVE
Monika

I can't believe I indulged in a piece of enchilada. Was it amazing? Yes, it was almost orgasmic. Speaking of, did I moan in front of Silas? For my sanity, I hope not. Facing him again would be mortifying if I did and he heard me.

Much to my dismay, all hear is Brandon's nagging voice in the back of my mind. *"Monika, you don't need that. You're fat enough."*

Brandon didn't always treat me badly, the first two years we were together were great. He was super supportive and always pampering me. It was only the last three years that his behavior toward me changed.

When I left the lounge earlier, Silas was back to his cold distant self. Which only amplifies Brandon's voice in my head. I know it sounds stupid, the two are completely different people and polar opposites. Yet, the way Silas wouldn't even look at me after I ate the food that he offered made me feel as small as Brandon used to make me feel.

This, my friends, is why I stay depressed.

My cell phone beeps with an incoming text. Glancing down, I see Amy has sent an attachment. Opening the message, I smile. It's a picture of her with her German Shephard, Gus. His tongue is hanging out of the side of his mouth and he's wearing the sweetest smile.

Amy and Gus ended up together through this clinic. Gus had

been brought in after he'd been hit by car. The couple that dropped him off couldn't take him in, and we could not locate the owner. When Amy heard that we would have to send him to the shelter, she came in and signed adoption papers. Now Gus is thriving, and Amy is in love.

Butch whines and I shut off my cell phone to tend to his needs. It's about time for his pain medicine. Just as I get up to administer that, Silas enters. The softer side of him I ate dinner with is long gone. Holding out his hand, he says, "I'll take care of the meds, go to my office and take a nap."

"I don't mind."

His hand grips my arm as I take a step toward the dog. My body instantly stiffens, expecting pain to follow. Three years with Brandon and his occasional physical lashings has trained my body to expect pain when grabbed a certain way. When no pain follows, I feel like a fool for reacting as such in front of Silas. "I said to take a nap." When I open my mouth to respond, he continues speaking. "It's nearly midnight. I have a cot out and ready. Just do as you're told and let me take over until Jose gets here."

I'm not sure if I'm more offended or relieved. Rather than argue and earning a spot on his shitlist, I place the medicine in his waiting palm and exit the room with a yawn. Honestly, I've been fighting to stay awake for the last couple hours.

Just like he said, there is a cot set up in the middle of his office, and by the looks of it, he also took a nap here. Toeing off my shoes, I lie down on the small cot. Pulling the blanket up, I catch a whiff of his cologne. Yep, he definitely took a nap here. Inhaling, I snuggle deeper into the comfort of the blanket. God, he smells so good.

It's easy to close my eyes when I'm all wrapped up in Silas. Well, not Silas but rather his scent. If I could bottle his fragrance —his cologne mixed with his natural scent—I would spray my pillow every night and sleep drowning in his essence.

Sunlight disturbs my dreams and forces my eyelids open. Pressing the blanket to my nose, I inhale, smiling. His scent is still strong on the fabric. A contented sigh passes my lips. Oh, to wake up to this fragrance every morning.

"Ahem." Freezing, I tug the blanket down and peer over at the desk where Silas is sitting behind his computer. "Care to share what you find so amusing down there?"

Oh. My. God. Did he hear me sniffing his blanket? I want to crawl under a rock and never come out. I'm sure he thinks I belong in an asylum. Suddenly, it dawns on me that the sun is shining brightly. "What time is it?"

"Nine o'clock."

Shooting up off the cot, I nearly fall flat on my face when it tips over with my movement. "What? Why did you let me sleep so long?" I struggle to get my shoes on my feet. "You were supposed to wake me when Jose arrived so I could go home. Now I'm late for my shift and have yet to shower."

I'm so worked up that I don't notice that Silas has stood and is closing the distance between us. Until he touches my shoulder. "Relax, Monika." Relax? How the hell am I supposed to relax when I'm needed out on the floor, and I'm still covered in yesterday's filth? "I'm giving you the day off."

No. I blanch at those words. Does this mean that he is gearing up to fire me? "What? Why?" I can't lose this job. I have worked far too hard to get where I am.

"Because you deserve it after last night." He urges me to gather my things and leave.

"Silas." When he lifts his eyebrow, I correct myself. "Doctor McKade, I can't afford to just take the day off."

Handing over my belongings, he says, "You'll be compensated. Now go home and get some proper rest." I open my mouth but close it immediately when he points toward the door, a no nonsense look on his face. "I'll see you tomorrow."

Dismissed, I walk out of the office and wave at Jose as we cross paths. Instead of driving home, I stop by the diner where Amy works. I could use a steaming cup of Joe. Taking a seat in the corner of Amy's section, I lean my head back and breathe a sigh of relief at the fact I get to relax today. And I get paid to do it.

Amy bounds over with coffee and a side of fruit. "Hey, you. What are you doing here at this time of day? Shouldn't you be at work?"

"I got the day off." I don't mention that her brother is paying me to take this time off.

"Good, I'm sure you need it after last night." She plucks a strawberry from my bowl and chews. "What are you eating this morning?"

I order my usual which is an egg white omelet with spinach, tomatoes, and mozzarella. No hash browns or bread. This is the option with the least number of calories. Then when I get home, I can run on the treadmill to work off those calories.

Amy visits my table as often as she can between customers. When I finish eating, we make plans to hang out after her shift. That will give me enough time to clean the house and do some grocery shopping.

As I'm unlocking my car, I hear a familiar voice. "Always eating. That's why you can never lose weight." Spinning on my heel, I come face-to-face with Brandon. Hanging off his arm is a skinny blonde. Built just the way he likes them. "This is Millie, my girlfriend."

Of course, he wants to shove her in my face. She is everything I'm not. A size double zero, small perky breasts, and a gap the size of Texas between her thighs. "Lovely to meet you." I smile at her. It's not her fault that her boyfriend is a mean asshole.

To throw gasoline on the fire, he cups her face and kisses her with passion. Making a show of sticking his tongue down her throat. As if to remind me that no man will ever want me the way he does her. Reminding me that my weight is the reason he never kissed me like that.

Anger and hurt bubble to the surface, each fighting for dominance. I want to lash out, ram my fist into his nose and kick him in the shin. Hurting him just a fraction of what he's hurt me would feel so good. It wouldn't accomplish anything, but it would make me feel better knowing that I dished out a little of what he gave me.

Moaning into her mouth, he grabs her ass through her jeans and squeezes. Slivers of glass pierce my heart. Why is he so cruel? I think I'm going to be sick. And to think, I wasted five years of my life with this man. Five years I can never get back.

Opening his eyes, he smiles into the kiss when he sees the tears brimming in my eyes. Only then does he break the kiss. "Come on, babe, I want to buy my beautiful girlfriend breakfast." Taking her by the hand, he drags her toward the building. No, *good to see you*, or even a *goodbye*. I'm nothing but a distant memory.

With a heavy heart, I get into my car and drive. The streets are a blur through my teary eyes. The highway seeming to take forever as I drive back toward town. My heart aching. I don't realize where I'm driving until I park my car next to a black Audi. Silas's Audi, which is parked right outside his office window.

He must have heard me pull up because his broad form fills the window, and I feel a smidgen of relief just knowing he's on the other side of that glass watching me. I should back out and go home like he instructed me to, but I can't find the will to leave. It may sound ridiculous, but being near him, even from this distance, helps calm the storm brewing in my heart.

When we were kids and I was having an extra bad day, I would run next door and visit Amy. It wasn't Amy I wanted to be near, it was Silas. Just like then, I crave his presence to heal my bruised and battered heart.

I don't know when he moved, but I shriek when my car door is thrown open and Silas squats to be eyelevel with me. Gray pools scan my tear-streaked face. "What happened?"

The concern on his face does something to me and I break, more tears streaming down my cheeks, wetting the collar of my scrubs top. All these years, this is what I've wanted, what I've craved. His attention. But this is not how I wanted to gain it. I never wanted him to see me like this. Weak and broken.

Hands shaking, I insert my key back into the ignition. Before I can turn the key, Silas grips my hand, stalling my movements. "Talk to me. Did someone hurt you?"

Oh Silas, you have no idea.

I want to tell him about all the abuse I suffered at the hands of my ex-boyfriend. To reveal to him how broken and dead I feel inside. How the smile I give to everyone around me is not a reflection of myself, but rather a mask I wear to conceal the pain.

"I'm fine." Wiping the wetness from my face, I flip the visor down and check my appearance. Red blotches cover my cheeks and forehead, my eyes are puffy and red rimmed. In other words, I'm a hot mess.

Gripping my chin, he gently forces my gaze to his. "Obviously, you are not fine. Tell me what happened."

"It's nothing. I shouldn't have come here." The hand on my chin tightens. Not painfully, just enough to let me know he's serious. "It's fine, I just ran into my ex at the diner. After introducing me to his new girlfriend, he made a show of playing tonsil hockey with her. It's not a big deal."

Those stony gray eyes harden to ice and his nostrils flare. "He made out with his new girl in front of you?"

Closing my eyes, because it's too painful to look in to his, I nod. "Yes, right in front of my car while I was trying to leave."

When his hand leaves my chin, I figure he thinks I'm overreacting to the situation and is going to send me on my way. So, to say I'm shocked when he unbuckles my seatbelt and tugs me from the car is an understatement. Taking the keys from my shaky hand, he locks the car and ushers me in the building.

A couple of the volunteers openly stare. Jamie, the receptionist, stands after seeing the state I'm in but Silas gestures for her sit back down. Thankfully she obeys without question. I don't feel like giving answers right now. He guides me to his office and closes the door behind us.

His arm moves from my shoulder to my waist as he walks us to the loveseat in the corner of the room. "How long were you together?"

The last thing I expect to hear is questions about my relationship with Brandon. I figured Silas would bring me in here, hand me a tissue, and then send me on my way after my nerves have calmed enough to drive.

Instead, he sits next to me, holding my hand. "We were together for five years."

Whether he knows he's doing it, I have no clue, but Silas is caressing the back of my hand with his thumb. "That's a long time to be in a relationship." I nod in agreement. "How long ago did you break up?"

"A couple months ago."

He grunts. "I hate to break it to you, but you weren't dating a man, you were dating boy." Letting go of my hand, he wraps his arm around me and pulls me close, stroking my hair. "No man would feel the need to rub your face in his new relationship. That's the sign of a weak, pathetic, and insecure loser."

Those words are a balm to my wounded soul and my tears slowly begin to dry. Leaning into his embrace, I finally feel safe. A feeling I haven't known in three long years. It's nice to find safety and comfort in him.

Knowing he needs to get back to his furry patients, I wipe the remaining wetness from my face. "Thank you."

"That's what big brothers are for, comforting his sister's best friend." Cue the cold water. That was a splash of reality thrown in my face. And here I thought it was because he cared about me on some level. Maybe not as girlfriend material, but at least in a friendly way. Guess I was wrong.

SIX
Silas

Ever since Monika left my office, I have been in a bad mood. What kind of man treats a woman like that? A woman he spent five years with. He's lucky I don't know who he is because I wouldn't think twice about putting my fist through his nose.

No one at work questions me on my behavior, they carry on with their tasks, only speaking to me when necessary. It's a good thing they leave me alone because my anger levels have been nearly beyond manageable all day. I want to take all the hurt from Monika and give her peace and comfort in its place.

Thankfully we don't have any overnight patients tonight. Sleeping on the cot was bad, but sleeping on that loveseat after Jose arrived for the second shift last night absolutely killed my back and neck. Now I'm home, sitting on my sofa with a box of pizza on the coffee table, and an action movie streaming on the television. The heartbroken expression on Monika's face still haunts me. Still infuriates me.

The more I think about her, the more I want her. Not being able to have her is going to be torture, and a temptation that I'm not sure I can overcome. She's like new blossoms in Spring. Beautiful and inviting. How do I work with her and not kiss her?

A text lights up my screen.

> Amy: Monika's had a shit day. Come hang out with us. She needs some cheering up.

My sister is going to be the death of me. Inviting me to hang out with her and the siren herself. Fanning the flame is what she's doing. Keeping my distance is proving to be a challenge, and I've just moved back a few days ago. I knew I should have stayed in the city. Life would have been much easier if I had.

> Silas: Where?

I'm half hoping she won't answer.

> Amy: Andromeda.

> Silas: Is that the hole-in-wall bar on sixth and Seminole in Okmulgee?

I don't want to get dressed and make the drive over to the next town just to drink a few beers and joke around with my sister and her best friend. The best friend that awakens lust in me every time we're in a room together.

> Amy: That's the one.

Against my better judgement, I let her know I'm on my way.

> Silas: Getting my shoes on. See y'all soon.

> Amy: You're the best.

I doubt she would be singing my praises if she knew the filthy thoughts in my head right now concerning her childhood best friend. No, in fact, she would most likely kick me in the nuts and dump a bucket of scalding water over my head if she knew what thoughts are taking residence in my mind.

Stuffing my face with a slice of pepperoni pizza, I toss the crust in the box and close the lid. I strip out of my sweatpants and pull on a pair of black jeans, a fitted charcoal shirt, and slip into my Vans.

Music blares through the atmosphere when I walk into the small building. The bass is heavy, reminding me of the parties I attended back in high school. As I push my way through the crowd, a brunette with bright red lipstick hooks her arm through mine. "Hey, handsome, care to dance?"

I open my mouth to tell her no just as movement across the room catches my attention. It's Monika, and the instant her gaze lands on me, her already crestfallen face breaks. Betrayal shines in her blue orbs and she quickly turns her head.

The brunette, oblivious to the pain slicing through me at the sight of Monika's hurt expression, leans into me, brushing her breasts against my arm. "Or we can get out of here. What do ya say?"

Shaking her loose, I step back. "I say no." Not bothering to engage further, I continue through the crowd. Amy is trying to convince Monika to eat something, but the woman just shakes her head. Which angers me. I don't understand why she does this to herself.

Blowing out a frustrated breath, Amy leans back. That's when she sees me. A sad smile curves her lips. "Hey Silas."

"Hey." Sitting next to my sister, I smile over at Monika. "How are you doing?"

"Peachy." She lifts her hand, signaling the waitress. "I'll take another shot of Tequila, please." The waitress nods and waltzes toward the bar. A minute later, she sets a shot glass in front of Monika, asking the rest of us if we need anything. Amy declines and I order a bottle of Guinness.

Music changes and people gather on the dancefloor for line dancing. I've never been a fan of those types of dances, but to each their own. On a couple of occasions, the brunette from earlier waves her fingers at me as she passes by. Each time, red stains Monika's cheeks. I'm not sure if she's jealous or just pissy because of the way her ex treated her today. My money is on the latter of the two. There is no reason for her to be jealous. Unless she still has a crush on me.

The third time Ms. Brunette passes our table, she slips a note across the tabletop, leaning toward me. "Call me."

Needing to stop this before the situation escalates further, I take the note, crumbling it in my palm and hand it back to her. "Not interested. Leave me alone." Shock spreads on her face as she takes in my words and actions. Then she spins on her heel and flees.

Both women at the table stare at me with wide eyes. Monika's with surprise, probably not expecting me to turn down a pretty woman. Amy's with shock at the rudeness with which I spoke. "Damn, brother, that was cold."

Shrugging my shoulders, I say, "Well, I'm not interested. She didn't take the hint earlier so I decided to relay the message in a way I knew would get through."

I nurse my beer while the girls talk about Gus. Monika is slowly starting to come out of her funk. Thank God, because I can't stand to see her so sad. In the middle of gushing over her dog, Amy gets a phone call. "It's my neighbor, I'll be right back."

Flagging down our waitress, I order a large basket of fries. If Monika hasn't eaten much, and by the sounds of their conversation when I arrived, I don't suspect she has, she'll need food in her belly to help absorb the alcohol she's quickly consuming.

Amy rushes back to our table, snatching her purse off the seat. "Sorry, I have to go. Gus escaped the backyard. Luckily Von was able to catch him, but I need to get him inside."

"Okay, let me get my purse." Monika sets her margarita down and reaches for her belongings.

Figuring this means that the two rode to town together, I put my hand up. "Sit, you need food to go with all the alcohol you're consuming." Turning to my sister, I say, "I'll give her a ride back home. Go take care of your pet."

"You're the best." She kisses my forehead and waves to her friend.

Picking up her drink, Monika sips her frozen margarita. Seemingly unsure how to act in my presence. The feeling is mutual. I know exactly how I want to behave, territorial and handsy. Kissing her every chance I get. Unfortunately, we don't always get to have our cake and eat it too.

The basket of fries arrives and Monika's nostrils flare when she inhales the aroma. Based on our conversation last night about food, I'll bet everything I own that she has denied herself fries to keep with her caloric deficits.

"Go ahead." I nod toward the basket sitting between the two of us.

"I can't." Pointing to the now empty margarita glass, she sighs. "I've already drank my calories for the day, and then some."

This shit is starting to piss me off. The woman has no need to deprive herself the way she is. Her body is not overweight. In fact, she has the most appealing body I've seen in ages. "You need food to compensate for the alcohol." Picking up a fry, I offer it to her. "Now, eat up."

Hesitating, she bites her lip. She wants the fry, probably has been craving one since she began cutting calories. Shrugging, I pop the fry in my mouth. Her eyes follow the motion and I make a show of savoring the salty potato.

When I offer her the next one, she takes it. "Fine." Taking the fry, she brings it to her lips biting the end when a male voice makes her shrink back in the seat, dropping the fry back into the basket.

"And this is why you can't lose weight." A scrawny, darkhaired male stops next to our table. He makes a show of grabbing the flat ass of the blonde by his side. "French fries and margaritas will only add to your fat rolls."

Red tints Monika's cheeks and she looks away, pushing the basket of fries further away from her. "It was just one bite, Brandon. It's not like I was making a meal of it."

Why the hell is she trying to explain herself to this jerk?

This buffoon rolls his eyes. "One bite too many, if you ask me."

Standing, I say, "No one asked you."

His eyes finally cut to me. "And who the hell are you?"

Snatching Monika's purse from the seat, I reach for her hand, smiling when she places her palm in mine. "I'm the guy taking her home." I don't clarify that I'm just taking her home, and not *taking* her home.

Doubling over, Brandon bursts with laughter. "Yeah right. What do you have planned with that fat ass, cookies and ice cream?"

A surge of anger slithers through my veins. Did he just call her a fat ass? Is this what she endures, and the reason she watches her calorie intake? I'm not sure who this guy is but I am about two seconds away from punching him in the face.

Tugging the blonde under his arm, he faces Monika. "This right here is what a woman should look like." The blonde has the decency to look ashamed of his statement, as she should. "I'm so glad I don't share your bed anymore."

Tears spring to Monika's eyes and before the douchebag can see the effects of his words, I pull her up from her seat. Cupping her face in my hands, I bring my lips down on hers. Public affection isn't my thing, but for her, I'm throwing all caution to the wind and making a big show for this loser that's causing her pain.

Using my thumb to tug on her chin, I urge her to open her mouth. She does and I slide my tongue into her mouth, kissing her like my life depends on it. Brandon makes a comment about how disgusting our display is. Those words only spur me on, and I grab Monika's ass, bringing her flush against my body.

Moaning into the kiss, she wraps her arms around my neck. She tastes like mango and tequila. Threading her fingers through my hair, she fists the strands, and the action causes my dick to jump in my jeans. A gasp forces her lips to part from mine when she feels the effect that she has on me.

Pecking her lips one more time, I make sure to glance at Brandon as I speak to Monika. "Come on, sweetheart, let's finish this at home."

Brandon's mouth drops so wide, he'll probably catch flies.

Good, he deserves it. Especially if this is the ex that tormented Monika today and caused her to come to the clinic in tears. If he wants to play games. Fine. We'll play games.

SEVEN
Monika

The fries smell so good. I haven't eaten one in nearly two years and I'm dying to taste it. Just one. "Go ahead," Silas nods toward the basket of heaven sitting on the table between us.

I want one, I do, but Brandon's voice keeps me from enjoying what I crave most. Even now, two months after we've been broken up. "I can't." To emphasize why, I point at my empty glass with a sigh. "I've already drank my calories for the day, and then some."

What I want is to say forget it and eat the damn fries. I enjoyed life so much more back when I didn't care what others thought. Back before Brandon. After enduring his verbal abuse, all I can think about is my weight and how other men are disgusted by my body.

"You need food to compensate for the alcohol." Reaching for a fry, he holds it out to me. "Now, eat up."

War is raging in my spirit. Part of me is drooling while the other part is scolding. The devil on one shoulder, the angel on the other. Who will win? Will I be able to refrain and keep to my diet? I need to, especially if Silas is ever going to see me as an attractive woman. Which, let's admit, I still want that badly.

Shrugging his shoulders, he opens his mouth and shoves the fry in, chewing without a care in the world. He licks his lips and sucks the salt off each finger. I can't help but watch with wild fascination, imagining all the things he can do with that tongue.

Great, now I'm actively lusting for my best friend's brother.

Fruit and an egg white omelet are all I've eaten today, and that was this morning. It's nearly ten o'clock now. When he offers me the next fry, my stomach growls painfully. "Fine." I take the crinkle cut potato and bite into it, closing my eyes at the crunchy outer layer mixed with the soft inner.

Interrupting my blissful moment is Brandon's voice. "And this is why you can't lose weight." Old habits have me shrinking back in embarrassment, dropping the remaining fry into the basket. The moment I look up, Brandon grabs Millie's—I think that's her name—backside. "French fries and margaritas will only add to your fat rolls."

My cheeks burn with his words. It's bad enough when I'm alone, but this time he humiliates me in front of Silas. Oh God. Kill me now. How can I face this man every day after he's heard the way Brandon speaks to me? He must think I'm weak for not standing up to this bastard.

Unable to bear looking at either man, I turn my head, pushing the basket of fattening fries toward Silas. "It was just one bite, Brandon. It's not like I was making a meal of it." Here I am defending myself like his opinion still matters. Damnit, I'm an idiot.

Mentally, I can hear Brandon snort, the way he always did when he didn't approve of my food choices. "One bite too many, if you ask me."

When Silas stands, I think he is about to walk away and leave me here with my tormentor. Instead, to my relief, I hear, "No one asked you."

Hearing Silas stand up for me, I finally turn my attention to what's going on around me. Brandon's mean glare lands on Silas. "And who the hell are you?"

Silas leans forward, picking up my purse and holding his hand out to me. I sigh in relief at the realization he is taking me away from the one I hate the most. A smile graces his face when I slip my hand into his. Then he cuts his gaze toward Brandon. "I'm the guy taking her home."

With a hand on his stomach, Brandon doubles over and laughs hysterically. "Yeah right. What do you have planned with that fat ass, cookies and ice cream?" I never understood how he could be so cruel.

Silas's body stiffens and I swear I can feel him holding back from attacking my ex.

Tugging Millie under his arm, Brandon looks at me. "This right here is what a woman should look like." At least his girlfriend has the decency to look ashamed of her man's behavior. "I'm so glad I don't share your bed anymore."

Ouch. That stings.

Tears fill my eyes and blur my vision. Brandon's words are like a dagger to the heart. Slicing and dicing just like a chef in the kitchen. The hand holding mine pulls me to my feet and I'm glad Silas is going to get me out of here. I might die if I have to listen to one more word of Brandon's cruelty.

Cupping my face, I don't expect what happens next. Silas leans forward, pressing his lips to mine. They're soft and warm and comforting. And everything I've ever wanted. Gripping my chin, he presses on it with his thumb, and I open for him. Granting him the access he's requesting.

A tornado twists in my stomach when his tongue enters my mouth and snakes around mine. Brandon snorts and makes a nasty comment about how kissing me is disgusting. As if those words light a fire in Silas, he deepens the kiss and grabs my backside, squeezing like he can't get enough of me, and bringing me flush against his body.

Is this how a kiss is supposed to feel? I've only ever kissed Brandon and he never made me feel like this. Like my every cell is vibrating with electricity. I moan into Silas's mouth, and he swallows the sound as I wrap my arms around his neck.

Threading my fingers through his hair, I fist the strands. When I do, his dick jerks and I gasp from the feel of him. He's hard and thick, and pressing into my stomach. Is he enjoying this kiss as much as I am?

Relaxing his hold on me, he pecks me on the lips. When he speaks, he looks at my ex, but his words are directed at me. "Come on, sweetheart, let's finish this at home." I know he's saying this to piss off Brandon and I can't help but look to see what my ex will do next.

Brandon's mouth flops open wide enough to see the silver fillings coating his molars, and I bite my bottom lip to hide the smile creeping up. I'm glad Silas put on a show to get under Brandon's skin. I doubt it hurt him even a fraction of how he hurt me this morning, but it's a good start.

Flipping my ex-boyfriend the bird, I slip my arm through Silas's and follow him out the door. It felt damn good to kiss Silas. The few short minutes that his mouth moved against mine was absolute heaven. Kissing him was everything I always thought it would be, and so much more.

As we weave through the crowd, I am walking on cloud nine. Nothing could bring me down right now. For the first time in a long time, I don't care what others are thinking as they turn to stare at me. I don't care whether they consider me overweight or ugly.

I'm flying high on Silas and the rest of the world doesn't exist.

I'm not saying I will quit cutting carbs and cease counting calories. All I'm saying is that Silas's kiss washed away those self-conscious thoughts that are always screaming at me. His kiss wiped Brandon's words from my mind, at least for a little while.

Chilly night air is welcoming after spending the last couple of hours couped up in that packed bar. Although, I'm sure the heat in my cheeks has more to do with all the alcohol than the body heat.

The black Audi comes into view just as a hand grips my upper arm, jerking me from the safety that is Silas. It takes my brain far too long to register what is happening. I blame the Tequila flowing through my veins. Silas is not as slow to process as I am. He spins on his heel locking his steely gaze on the one holding me captive.

His hands fist at his sides, and Silas takes a step toward me and the one holding on to me. "What the hell do you think you're doing?"

It's now that I look up into the brown eyes that I once loved, or thought I loved. Brandon's nose crinkles and his grip on my arm tightens, almost painfully. "I should be asking you that question, don't you think?"

"Brandon, let go." I try to jerk my arm out of his hold, but the attempt is futile.

"No." My ex forcefully tugs on my arm until my body trips into his. "What the hell was that display back there?"

"Brandon, please." Of their own accord, tears spring to my eyes, trailing down my cheeks and dripping onto the collar of my shirt. "Please don't make a scene."

"Why?" He's shouting now. Always shouting when I've pushed him too far. "Because you're the only one allowed to make a scene?" I open my mouth to respond. To tell him I wasn't making a scene, but he doesn't give me the opportunity. "Or is it because you don't want everyone to see how pathetic you are. In fact, I bet you paid him good money to kiss you."

"No, that's not true." Why the hell am I explaining anything to him? It's none of his business what I do. Not anymore.

"That's it isn't it?" Brandon's nostrils flare and his eyes darken to near black. A sign that he is point two seconds away from losing his cool and becoming physical.

"I'm warning you." Silas takes another step toward us. "Let her go."

Anger has blinded Brandon to the point he isn't listening to anyone other than himself. "You paid some stranger to kiss you in front of me to make me jealous." I shake my head because that's not true. "News flash, Monika, no man will ever want a fat ass like you. Not me, and damn sure not that man you were with."

"That's it." Silas rears back and punches Brandon in the face. Not once but four times. Between punch two and three, Brandon loses his grip on me. Thank God. After the fourth punch, my ex doubles over, groaning in pain. Judging by the blood pouring out of Brandon's nose, I'd say it's broken. "I told you to let her go." Silas wraps an arm around my waist. "Not that it's any of your damn business. Monika didn't pay me a dime. I kissed her because she is the most beautiful woman on the planet. Now, if you'll excuse us, I want to get my girl home."

Once we get in the car, Silas helps me buckle the seatbelt because my hands are too shaky to snap the metal piece into place. And for the second time tonight, Brandon embarrassed me in front of the one person I wish hadn't witnessed it.

EIGHT
Silas

What in the ever-loving hell was that? That man had a girlfriend by his side when he entered that bar, yet he followed us outside to try and stake some kind of claim on Monika. And the way she coward down when he spoke to her. I've seen that fear before. Her reaction is that of an abused wife. This pisses me off something fierce. So pissed off, I'm seeing red.

Those days are over if I have anything to say about it. I will not stand by while any man puts his hands on a woman. Especially when that woman is Monika Grayson. Without question, I will walk through the fires of hell to protect this sweet woman currently sitting in my passenger seat.

Once her seatbelt is in place, I pinch her chin to bring those baby blues my way. "You're safe now." Her entire body is shaking and my heart breaks for her. "I'm taking you home with me." Her eyes widen like saucers. "You shouldn't be alone right now." Brushing loose strands of hair out of her face, I gently caress her cheek. "Let me take care of you tonight, okay?"

When she blinks, fresh tears fall. "Okay." It's just a whisper, but it's all I need. Wiping her face with the pads of my thumbs, I marvel at the strength of this woman. To have gone through what I suspect she has, and still present herself as confidant, is not for the faint of heart.

Reversing out of the parking spot, kicking up dirt on that dickhead sill lying on the ground, I head toward the highway that will take us home. Inside I'm fuming. I would rather be standing out there pounding out my anger on her loser of an ex. The most important thing right now is not giving him what he deserves but tending to a very vulnerable Monika.

All during our drive, I'm wondering if Amy knew what kind of man this Brandon guy is. In all these years, my sister has never once told me that her best friend was in trouble. Granted, our conversations didn't exactly stray toward Monika. Every once in a while, Amy would drop little details about her best friend. Like when her father passed away in a sky diving accident. Ninety-nine percent of the time, our conversations were family related.

If she knew and did nothing to help her friend out of a dangerous situation, I will be furious with my sister. I thought she loved Monika. Not helping her out of a relationship like that is not how you love your friends.

I'm seething by the time I pull into my driveway. Shutting off the engine, I get out fully intending on walking around to open her door for her, but she is already standing at the front of my car. The tears have dried up, but she is still a shell of the woman I've seen the last few days.

She must sense what is simmering under my skin because she bows her head and shrinks back. "I'm sorry."

"What the hell are you sorry for?" I immediately regret voicing that in a stern tone when I see her lifting her shoulders to her ears and cowering further. It's not her I'm angry with, it's him, but seeing her like this is ice to the fire in my veins. "Shit, I'm sorry Monika."

"It's okay." Wrapping her arms around her middle, she starts walking toward my house, leaving me to trail after her. Her steps are fast, and she never once lifts her head.

When we reach the front door, I step beside her and slide my key into the lock, opening the door for her to enter. Only, she doesn't move from her spot. "Are you coming inside?" I sweep my arm toward the open doorway, inviting her into my home.

"Yes." The word is but a whisper.

"Okay." I wait a few seconds but when she still hasn't moved, I ask, "What are you waiting for?"

"You."

This leaves me more confused than ever. "What do you mean?"

Now those blue doe eyes peer up at me. "Don't you want to enter first?"

Huh? "Why would I enter first? What kind of a man would I be if I didn't let the ladies in first?"

She shrugs like that is a foreign concept for her. I know it's not because her father was an old school gentleman. "I'm sorry." Again, with the *I'm sorry*. Since we've been working together, I don't think I've ever seen this side of her. Did running into her ex set her back into old habits?

Placing my hand on the small of her back, I gently guide her over the threshold. Once we are both in, I turn the deadbolt and flip on the lights. Her gaze wanders the interior of my home, soaking everything in. "How about some coffee and pizza?" I still have the large pepperoni pizza I had just opened before my sister summoned me to entertain her friend.

"I'm not sure about the coffee." Turning so we're face-to-face, she shrugs. "The caffeine will keep me up."

Guess I've built an immunity to it, I tend to drink coffee day and night without it effecting my sleep. Good news for her, the office is closed tomorrow, so if it did disrupt her sleep, it wouldn't be a big deal. "We're not open tomorrow, I think you'll be fine."

Those ruby lips tip up in a small smile. "Right." Seeing the coat hooks by the front door, she hangs her purse. "In that case, I'd love some coffee."

Nothing is said about the pizza, but I'm warming her a slice anyway. As I set about brewing coffee and warming food, I watch as she takes her shoes off, placing them next to the front door. My need to protect stems from events of our past. For as long as I've known her, I've had this overwhelming need to take care of her.

Of course, it was all done in secret from her. Just me playing the part of big brother.

As soon as there is enough coffee in the pot, I pour two mugs and grab the plate with four slices of pizza. Setting the plate on the coffee table, I hand her a mug. She smiles. "Thank you." Picking up a slice, I offer it to her. "Oh, I can't, but thank you."

"You can." Holding the pizza to her mouth, I urge her to take a bite. "Your body needs sustenance." Her gaze lands on her stomach and she shakes her head. This pisses me off because she has no reason to deny herself the foods she desires. Moving off the sofa, I squat down in front of her so she can see me. "Get that asshole out of your head. His words were vicious and a lie. There's not a damn thing wrong with your body." Putting the pizza back to her lips, I say, "Now, eat."

Studying me—for what, I'm not sure—she finally opens her mouth and takes the tiniest bite. It's not what I was hoping for, but it'll do. For now. "Thank you."

"No need to thank me." I watch her blow on the steaming java in her hand, then sip the hot liquid. Out of nowhere, my body reacts, remembering the feel of those lips from not so long ago. Mentally shaking my head, I do my best to squash those thoughts before the evidence of my lust shows. Moving back to the sofa, I once again hold out the slice of pizza. "Eat." This time she bites off a bigger piece. "Good girl."

Bringing the slice to my own mouth, I consume three times the size. Her blue orbs track the movement of my tongue as I lick sauce off my lips. If I didn't know better, I'd say she wants me just as much as I want her.

What I'm about to do is playing with fire. It's the one thing I should not do. Yet here I am going for the one thing I want more than anything. The forbidden fruit. Monika. This particular fire may just get me burned. But, damn, it'd be worth it.

Tossing the mostly eaten pizza back onto the plate, I lean toward her, plucking a strand of that blonde hair and running it through my fingers. "Do you know how beautiful you are?" I can see it in her eyes, she doesn't believe a word I say.

"You don't have to say that." Closing her eyes, she says, "I know I'm not what men want."

Jeez, that's some number he did on her. For her to believe that no man will want her. Bullshit. I want her. So much so that I'm willing to play with fire and risk getting burned. "That's a lie, sweetheart." Sweeping her hair from her neck, I trail kisses from her collarbone up to the shell of her ear. "Men do want you." I pepper her jaw with kisses until I reach her lips. "I want you."

Cupping her face with both hands, I angle her head just right and press my lips to hers. Unlike earlier in the bar, her body is stiff and she's clutching that cup of coffee like it might save her from danger. No worries, sweetheart, there's no danger here. Not with me. I take the cup from her hands and place it on the coffee table.

"Come here." I lean back and pat my lap.

Biting her bottom lip, she stares at my legs. "I can't, I'm too heavy."

"Push him out of your head." Taking her hand, I tug, urging her on. "You're not too heavy. You're just right." It takes her longer than I'd like, but she finally shifts closer, straddling me. Slipping my hand into her hair, I guide her forward for another kiss. This time, she opens and grants me access to her mouth.

Our tongues move together, and her body slowly melts into mine. Yet, I can tell she is still trying to keep most of her weight off me. That won't do. I want all of her. Figuring she needs me to help her fully fall into this moment, I reach up with my free hand and pinch her nipple through the fabric of her shirt. It instantly hardens between my fingers, and she gasps into my mouth.

If it takes me all night, I will show her how desirable she is.

This time when I pinch her nipple, I roll that bud between my fingers the best I can through her clothing. She arches back and I release her breast to grip her hip, pressing down at the same time I thrust upward. "You feel that?" Her moan echoes in the otherwise quiet room. "This is the reaction of a man who desires you." To prove my point, I repeat the action.

Wrapping both arms around my neck, she leans forward, taking my lips. This time she gives in to her wanton needs, grinding onto my erection. Our breathing turns into pants as we move our bodies together. My hand on the back of her neck tightens and I dominate her mouth in a bruising kiss. Moaning, she moves her hips faster, seeking a release that I'm sensing is vastly approaching.

Slipping my hand under her shirt, I pull the cup of her bra down and squeeze her soft breast. If I thought her nipple was hard before, it's granite now. All it takes to tip her over the edge is a tweak and a roll of that rock-hard pebble. Her body shakes and she breaks our kiss, burying her face in the crook of my neck, moaning, and grinding against me.

Damn, I barely touched this woman and she fell apart for me. Forget the coffee and pizza, I grip her under the thighs and stand. On instinct, Monika wraps her legs around my waist. Worry crosses her features, and I can tell by the way she's nibbling on her lip that she fears her weight is an issue. It's not, she's much lighter than she thinks.

The bedroom door is only partially closed, so I kick it open and take her straight to the bed. She scoots up to the middle and watches me with a mixture of lust and disbelief. Believe it, sweetheart. This is happening.

I reach behind me, ripping my shirt over my head and tossing it to the floor. Blue eyes rake over my body and she licks her lips like she wants to devour me. Good, I feel the same. Tonight, I'm going to worship her body the way it should be.

Climbing onto the bed, I use my knee to part her thighs. They fall open, but not open enough for my liking. Leaning down, I kiss her deeply. The more I kiss her, the farther her legs fall apart. With one hand, I unbutton her jeans, slipping my hand beneath the fabric to rub her sensitive flesh. "Silas." My name is a half moan, half whisper.

"What do you want, sweetheart?" She doesn't answer, but her hips buck against my palm, seeking friction. I give her what she wants, moving my palm in circles while inserting a finger into her core.

Our kiss turns hurried as she reaches yet another climax. I smile against her lips, then sit on my heels so I can tug her jeans from her body. Her pink lace panties are next to hit the floor. She is beautiful laying on my bed, naked from the waist down. Blonde locks fanning my pillow.

My hands land on her thighs and I slide them up her body and under her shirt. When I gather the hem in my hands and push the material upward, she halts my movements. "Wait."

Looking up at her, I wonder if she has changed her mind about moving to the next base. "Second thoughts, sweetheart?"

"No." She averts her gaze and chews on that bottom lip. Always with the bottom lip, and it's sexy as hell. "I just...I mean... Wouldn't you rather leave the top on?"

Leave the top on? On what universe would a guy not want his woman completely naked in his bed? "No, sweetheart, I would not rather leave the top on." Inching the material further up, I keep my eyes fixed on hers as I reveal her breasts. "I want all of you." To quiet her nerves, I glance down at her and lick my lips. "You are so beautiful." Tossing her shirt to the floor, I unfasten her bra and drop it to the side of the bed. Allowing my gaze to linger, I soak in those exquisite breasts. "Your body is perfection."

NINE
Monika

Shock waves wrack my body, and my skin is flaming hot. The only man I have ever been with was Brandon and he never took care of me the way Silas is, and we haven't even had sex yet. It's like he knows I have been denied the fulfillment of passionate sex and is trying to make it up to me.

When the tremors start to fade, his palms fall to my inner thighs, caressing the tender flesh in circular motions. Inching higher, the ghosting of his fingertips on my lower abdomen sends shivers through my body. Before I know what he is doing, he gathers the hem of my shirt and starts pushing the material upward.

That old voice in the back of my head speaks loudly in my mind.

Leave that shirt on, why on earth would I want to look at your fat body while we have sex?

Look at all those rolls, why can't you just have a sexy body?

Fear shoots through me like a rocket and I grip what I can of the shirt and try to tug it back down. What will he think if he sees my soft belly and triple D breasts? Brandon never liked my breasts. Said they were too heavy and not perky enough. "Wait."

Concern shines in his eyes and he stills his movements. I know I'm about to ruin this moment and I hate myself for it. "Second thoughts, sweetheart?" Even though I'm acting like a crazy person, he is still just as sweet.

In this moment, I'm glad I'm not dealing with asshole Silas. "No." How the hell do I communicate this to him? Averting my gaze, I take a deep breath as I try to find the words. Several phrases flit through my mind but none of them feel right. I have a feeling I am going to run him off and then I'll be left looking for work elsewhere. Guess there's no better way than coming right out with it. Like ripping a band-aide off. "I just...I mean... Wouldn't you rather leave the top on?"

So many different emotions flash across his face. Not a single one of them I recognize. I'm nervous. Up to this point I have enjoyed myself, but things have the potential to go south, and fast. Just when the silence is about to consume me, he speaks. "No, sweetheart, I would not rather leave the top on."

Does he even know what he's asking for? I'm sure Silas has had many women in his bed over the years. Women who are skinny and fit the porno profile, just like Brandon prefers. I am not that woman. My body is soft, and I have love handles right on my hips.

Inching the material further up, his gaze never leaves mine. His movements are slow, and his fingers leave goosebumps in their wake. When the fabric slips over my breasts, his thumbs brush against my nipples. "I want all of you."

I want to believe him, I do, but all my insecurities are overwhelming me. Screaming at me that I'm not good enough.

Slowly, ever so slowly, his gaze trails down my body and he licks his lips. "You are so beautiful." His hands keep pushing upward. I get the hint and lift so he can pull the shirt from my body. While I'm in this position, he quickly unhooks my bra with one hand—I'm not going to fret over how much practice he's had to get that good—and tosses it to the side. Hungry eyes linger on my breasts. "Your body is perfection."

Words I never thought I would hear from a man's mouth. Hearing them from Silas stirs so many emotions within me, I'm not sure how to react. But the one thing I didn't think would happen are the tears that spring forth.

To make matters worse, a strangled noise builds in the back of my throat as I try to hold back a sob. Silas looks up, those gray eyes softening. "Hey, what's all this?" He brushes away the tears. His gentleness brings on a whole new wave of tears and I want nothing more than for the earth to swallow me whole. "What's with the tears?"

Humiliation and relief fill me at the same time. Humiliation over the fact I have no control over these blasted tears and am making a fool of myself. Relief that he isn't running for the hills, demanding I leave and never return. "I just never thought I'd hear those words."

Furrowing his brows, he asks, "What words?"

Now I'm too embarrassed to carry on this conversation with him. "Never mind, I'm sorry for being such a mess."

"Hey." He cups my face and kisses me tenderly. "You are not a mess." Trailing his finger down my neck, across my breast, and over my belly, he stops at the apex of my thighs. "If your previous boyfriends haven't told you how beautiful you are, then they are blind and stupid."

"Boyfriend."

Arching a brow, he appears confused. "What?"

"I've only had one boyfriend. Only ever been with one man." I don't know why I feel the need to correct him. Maybe a part of me wants him to know that I'm not a slut. Sleeping around is not my thing.

Shaking his head, he places a kiss on my nose. "That train wreck is not a man." Then his fingers skirt between my folds, playing with the most sensitive part of me. "A man does not insult, nor does he instill fear in his woman." His hand leaves my body long enough to unbutton his jeans and push them down, kicking them off. Placing a foil packet between his teeth, he rips it open, rolling the latex down his length. "A man treats his woman like a queen." On the last word, he thrusts inside me and the two of us moan in unison.

Holy shit, he feels good. So good. It's like my body just came alive with that single thrust. The intrusion is heavenly and lights my body on fire.

Silas is much bigger than what I'm used to, also much gentler. Brandon never eased into me, he just rammed in and rutted until he reached his climax, then rolled over and went to sleep. He was always a wham-bam-thank-you-ma'am kind of guy. Only without the thank you.

This is a whole new experience. Silas pumps his hips and grinds against me in a way that causes my vaginal walls to flutter. His lips find mine and we kiss, breathing each other in as our bodies fit together in the most perfect way.

Sensations unlike I've known tear through me. Tightening in my abdominal muscles has me arching my back and bucking against him without abandon. I break the kiss because I'm not sure I can take much more. My thighs start to shake as Silas grinds against me again and again. "Fall apart for me. Let me see how beautiful you look when you come."

His words are my undoing and a climax, so fierce, rocks through me. Resulting in involuntary convulsions. Words are whispered against my mouth but I'm too high on him to comprehend them. Silas is one drug I never want to give up. The one addiction I would happily keep.

"Yes." His hips pump faster, his teeth nipping my earlobe. "You feel so good." Bowing his head, he thrust three more times and then stills. His dick hardens further and then pulses. Those pulses extend my orgasm and have me gasping for breath.

Silas rests his head against my shoulder, and I turn my head so I can kiss his temple.

We stay in the same position until he softens inside me. Running his nose along my jaw is the most intimate thing I've experienced. Well, other than what we just did. He peppers kisses on my neck and behind my ear. The events of the day combined with the alcohol I drank earlier finally hit me. My eyelids grow heavy, and a yawn stretches my mouth wide. As much as I would like to stay awake, I don't think I can last another minute.

Silas chuckles. "I'll be right back." I hum in acknowledgement. Seconds later he's back with a wet rag and to my embarrassment, he cleans me up. After discarding the rag in the laundry room, Silas slips into bed, snuggling in behind me. "Sleep. I'll take you home in the morning."

Spooning. I have never spooned with anyone in my life. Okay, I take that back. Amy and I have woken up spooning as teenagers. But that was because we had been camping in early spring and it had gotten chilly overnight. During sleep we must have been seeking heat and ended up curled into one another.

One arm slips under my head, the other drapes over my side and tugs my back flush against his front. He throws a leg over mine and kisses the back of my neck. No more words are spoken, and it doesn't take long to fall captive to sleep.

TEN
Silas

Reality hits hard when I open my eyes the next morning and see a text on my phone from my sister.

> Amy: Hey, thanks for taking care of Monika last night. You're the best big brother.

If only she knew how well I took care of Monika. What the hell did I do? And I can't even blame it on the alcohol because I barely touched the one beer I had. I did the one thing I swore I would never do. Fall into bed with my sister's best friend. A childhood best friend that is younger than me. Although, I suppose our four-year age difference doesn't really matter now that we're adults. Not to mention, she is my employee. Which is a major no-no.

Shit.

I pray Monika isn't the clingy type, or easily attaches emotionally, because this has to stop here. We cannot continue down this road. I did not move back to my hometown and take over a clinic just to throw it all away.

Getting out of bed, I gather my clothes and head to the guest room to shower. I need to get as far away from Monika as I can so I can clear my thoughts, and my lust. Going out last night was a huge mistake. A mistake that could ruin my relationship with my sister as well as ruin her relationship with her best friend.

Locking the bedroom door, I hop into the guest shower and crank up the hot water. I need to find a way to break this to Monika gently. The last thing I need is to run her off and lose the only good technician I have at the clinic. Who knows how long it would take to find a replacement in a town as small as this? Patient care would suffer without the aid of a technician.

Yes, I know I have two other technicians that help out on occasion, but she's working hard to gain her veterinarian degree and I can't lose talent like that.

The shower is hot, releasing tension from my neck and shoulders. Who knew that fretting over sleeping with your sister's best friend, and your employee, would cause such tightness in the muscles back there?

While washing my body, I rehearse the conversation that needs to be had in a hundred different ways. In each scenario, I envision Monika slapping me across the face and running to my sister. Damn, why didn't I think this through before I acted on my carnal desires? I have no one to blame but myself for the mess I'm in.

Shutting off the water, I dress and try to mentally prepare myself to face Monika. This can go one of two ways, and I have a feeling it will go the worst possible way. Why? Because that seems to be my luck.

Taking a deep breath, I unlock the door and quietly trek down the hall to my bedroom, ready to start this painful conversation. Except, when I enter, the bed is empty. Neatly made, but completely void of the woman I left sound asleep and wrapped in the cozy comforter.

A peek into the master bathroom shows that Monika is not there either. Dumping my dirty clothes into the hamper, I trek down the hall and come to a screeching halt in the kitchen when I spot Monika sitting at the island with a cup of coffee in hand.

Without meeting my gaze, she slides a plate across the granite. Eggs, bacon, and a side of fruit. "We need to talk."

Well, that's a first. I'm usually the one to start a conversation with those four words. It's a bit awkward to be on the receiving end of that phrase. "I agree." I eye Monika's plate, happy to see she made herself eggs as well. Egg whites, but at least she's eating protein along with her fruit.

She picks at her eggs, taking the tiniest bites between sips of coffee. Silence fills the atmosphere, and the only sound is our chewing. Out of all the women I've eaten with, this is the most uncomfortable I have ever been. And I've had some pretty damn uncomfortable moments in the past.

When I can't take the silence any longer, I set my fork down and prepare to get this over with. "So, last night—"

"Was a mistake," she cuts in.

My mouth flops open. That's a first. Never has a girl told me that I was a mistake. It's usually me that has to be the bad guy and break the news to her. Being on this side of the dumping fence sucks. Big time. Even though I came in here prepared to say the same thing to her, it stings being the one told.

Nibbling a strawberry, she continues to stare at her blank cell phone as she speaks. "Don't get me wrong, last night was amazing." She inhales and blows it out slowly. "Honestly, it was everything I hoped it would be, and more." Finally lifting her head, I see the unshed tears in her eyes and damnit if I don't want to go over there and wipe them from her face and kiss it all better. "But I love Amy more than I love myself, and this would wreck our friendship. I would never do that to her. Nor would I want to strain the relationship between the two of you."

If I didn't have a pull to this girl before, I damn sure do now. Her selflessness is a beacon to my soul. I wish there was a way around this stupid unspoken law that says *no dating your sister's best friend* and *no sleeping with your staff*. "You're a good friend."

What the hell was that? *You're a good friend.* That's the best I could come up with? Lame.

"Thanks." She looks as awkward as I feel. "I hope this doesn't change our working relationship. I would hate to lose a job that means so much to me. I've worked hard to get where I am."

She thinks I would fire her over something I initiated? Shaking my head, I push my now empty plate away and drain the last of my coffee. "Absolutely not. Your job is secure." I want to tell her how amazing she is at what she does, but I don't want to make this more difficult than it already is.

"Good." Seemingly satisfied, at least where her job is concerned, she scoops up the last of her egg whites and stacks her plate on top of mine, carrying them to the sink.

There is no way I'm letting her wash the dishes, especially since she was kind enough to cook for me. Catching her hand midway to the soap, I sandwich it between my much larger ones. "Leave the dishes, I'll take care of them later."

"Okay." Shoulders slumped and head down, Monika turns to leave.

Not wanting her to leave thinking she meant nothing, I tighten my grip on her hand. Her sad eyes meet mine and I about lose all my good sense. The need to pull her into my arms is strong. So strong that I have to fight hard to resist.

The battle is nearly lost, but at the last second, I'm able to overcome the urge to hold her tight and take her back to bed. "Last night may have been a mistake, but don't think for one minute that I regret it."

Blinking those sad eyes, a tear escapes and I swipe it away with the pad of my thumb. "You don't?"

If she needs assurance, I will give it to her. "I don't." Taking her chin between my fingers, I lean forward so our noses touch. "From the day I laid eyes on you, I've felt a pull toward you."

"You did?"

I nod. "You were just a kid, and I didn't know what to make of it, but I did my best to protect you while I lived at home." She doesn't know the extent of my protectiveness, and I don't need her to. "This was bound to happen. You're a beautiful woman and being with you was amazing."

"For me too." Tears mist her eyes once more and she blinks them away. "From the first day I saw you, sweaty and wearing your soccer gear, I wanted nothing more than to be your girl." Gripping my shirt in her fists, she tilts her head until our lips touch. The kiss is sweet and over too quickly. "Last night will be a memory I cherish for the rest of my life."

After Monika, I doubt I will ever find a woman that makes me feel as whole as she made me feel last night. But fantasy and reality cannot mesh, and the moment she walks out that door, we go back to what we were before.

As if on cue, her cell phone rings. Picking up the device, she answers the call. "Hey, Amy."

My sister? Shit.

"Skating? I don't know, it's been years since I've been to the rink." There's a pause while she listens to my sister. "Oh, he is? Okay, um, sure." Another pause. "I'll see you tonight then. Love you, bye."

Who is this *he* they were talking about? Is my sister trying to set Monika up on a date? The thought turns my stomach sour, but we already agreed that what happened last night was a one-time thing. We aren't together and cannot be together. So, if she decides to date, then its none of my business.

Then why do I feel a stab of jealousy just thinking about it?

Monika tosses her phone into her purse, a tight smile on her face. "Looks like I'll see you tonight?"

I'm about to ask what she means, but the vibration of the cell phone in my back pocket distracts me. Pulling it free, I glance down at the text message that appears.

> Amy: Skating tonight. Don't bail. See you at seven.

What the hell?

Well, at least I know the *he* that Monika was talking about with my sister. Skating is a sport I haven't participated in since high school. I'm not even sure I still have the coordination to glide across the rink.

"Bye, Mr. McKade." Monika opens the front door to leave. Though, she doesn't go past the threshold as her gaze lingers on my driveway. "Um, could I bother you for a ride home?"

I bite my cheek to keep from smiling. Looks like I'll get to spend a few more minutes with my siren.

ELEVEN
Monika

Amy bursts through my front door. Why? Because she has a key. Though she could have texted to say, *hey, I'm here*. She does what she always does. Come through that door like the fires of hell are chasing after her.

"Monika?" It's highly possible that the neighbors three blocks away can hear her shout my name.

"Right here." Clicking the off button on the television remote, I wave from my spot on the sofa. "Though with that voice, I'm sure every Monika in town turned their heads, wondering who is calling after them."

A laugh spills from her ruby red mouth as she rushes to me. "Hurry." Grabbing my hand, she tugs me to my feet and drags me out the door.

Amy is downright giddy tonight. So giddy, I'm wondering if there's a guy she's hoping to run into at the rink. "Jeez, slow down a bit." Getting into the passenger seat, I ask, "You have a date or something?"

Her smile is wide. "Yeah, or something." Then she backs out of the driveway and takes off toward the highway. It's a fifteen-minute car ride and we sing the whole way there. Neither of us is great, but in moments like these, girls just want to have fun.

The parking lot isn't huge, so it's easy to spot the black Audi from the street. I was half hoping that Silas would stay home tonight. Or at least not come to the skating rink. Looks like he can say no to his sister about as well as I can.

Getting through this night without giving Silas puppy dog eyes is going to be a challenge. Hell, working with the man may end up being the death of me. Oblivious to my dilemma, Amy tucks her arm in mine and struts toward the building.

Inside, Silas is leaning against the wall, arms crossed. "It's about time you showed. You sure you want to stick around with all these screaming teens?"

Before Amy opens her mouth to respond, the lights come on full force. From the overhead speakers comes an announcement. "Alright, minors, turn in your skates and make your way to the exit. Thank you for visiting Skate Fun. Come back and see us."

We watch as all the teenagers exit, giggling, a few couples are holding hands. Silas and I share a look, both uncertain what is going on. Then Amy cuts in. "Tonight, is adult night. No one under the age of twenty-one is allowed in."

Well, isn't that interesting. I didn't know they had such a thing. Back when we were kids, there was no adult night. "How did you even know about this?" Silas and I ask at the same time.

"Oh, Ronnie told me about it this morning." She shifts from one foot to the other.

I lift a brow because I'm not sure who this Ronnie is. "Who is Ronnie?" The name isn't familiar.

Nodding for us to follow her, she answers over her shoulder. "He's the new cook at the diner."

Vaguely, I remember her mentioning a new cook. We are the first in line to rent our skates. The girl behind the counter makes googly eyes at Silas and it takes everything in me to keep from launching over the counter and punching her in the stomach.

With the way she keeps her focus on Silas, I'm surprised she is able to get our skate sizes correct. Opening my purse, I retrieve my wallet but as I look up, Silas is swiping his debit card, paying for the three of us. That small gesture takes me back ten years. Back when Amy and I were eighth graders and Silas would drop us off and pay our way.

The girl scribbles on the receipt then hands it to Silas. "My name is Lacey, I wrote my number on the back, call me sometime."

How dare she? Taking a deep breath, I let it out through my nose. I can't let this get to me. But then Silas does the one thing that stabs me straight in the heart. He smiles at her, winking. "Thanks, darlin'." Flipping the receipt over, he studies the number then tucks it into his wallet.

Just because he kept the receipt, doesn't mean he is keeping her number. I know that in my head, but my heart sinks anyway, and I stumble over my own two feet. Blindly, I follow Amy to a bench where we trade our street shoes for the skates. Afterward, we find a locker and stuff our purses and shoes inside. To secure our items, she locks it with a padlock she brought from home.

Silas is already on the floor, skating circles around the rink. Skating to the bar, I order a shot of tequila, tossing it back and hissing through the burn. This is going to be a long night. Amy takes my hand, and we glide onto the smooth floor together. The song currently playing is a pop song from the nineties. It doesn't take long for muscle memory to kick in and I let go of Amy's hand to skate backward.

When I pass Silas and catch his stare, I turn back around and continue bopping my head and body to the beat of the music. A couple of guys skate up next to me and compliment me on my technique. I thank them and keep moving.

Two more songs and the DJ calls out for couples. Since I'm flying solo, I make my way to the sidelines. I could go for an ice-cold water. Just as my skates land on the blue carpet, Amy calls my name. She is standing with a broad-shouldered guy with a mop of blonde hair.

The two of them meet me halfway. Amy grins. "Monika, this is Ronnie. Ronnie this is the girl I was telling you about."

Telling him about? What was she telling him about me?

He holds out his hand and I place mine in his. "Nice to meet you."

"You too."

Instead of letting go of my hand, he tucks it into the crook of his arm. "Care to skate with me?" He's already leading me out onto the floor so it's not like I have much of a choice. The song that plays next is a slow, romantic song and Ronnie threads his fingers with mine as we take off. "You're pretty."

Um, awkward. "Thanks." I've known this man for less than a minute and he's already turning on the charm. Maybe it wouldn't bother me so much if I hadn't just spent the night with Silas last night. Then again, Silas did flirt back with the girl behind the counter. Still, it feels wrong to be skating to such a song with this man that I don't even know.

"Amy tells me you work with animals." He flips around, skating backward while holding both of my hands.

"I do. I'm a technician at the Morris Veterinarian clinic."

"That's so cool." Ronnie comes back to my side. He talks about his work at the diner, but I don't hear a word he says because my focus is on the guy currently staring daggers at the man by my side.

As we get close to where Silas is standing with his sister, his gaze sweeps over me, heating my body from head to toe. A shiver races down my spine and the corner of Silas's lips turn up. He knows exactly what his gaze has done to me.

When the song ends, Ronnie and I join Amy and Silas at a nearby table. There is a pitcher of Coke in the center and two extra cups. I take one of the plastic cups, filling it with the dark liquid. This will be the first soda I've consumed in ages. The coolness feels like heaven going down and helps lower my body temperature.

Ronnie scoots so close to me on the bench seat that our legs touch. Silas glares at Amy's friend like he would love to knock him out. Good. That's how I felt about the brazen woman that gave him her phone number without even asking if he was available.

A guy in an apron wanders over, carrying a tray of nachos in one hand and a tray of wings in the other. Both trays are set in the center of our table and Ronnie digs in without saying a word. I reach for a nacho at the same time Silas does. Not that I plan on eating that chip, I just need something for my fingers to do so I'm not admiring the man in front of me like a lovesick puppy. Our fingers brush against one another and it takes all I have, not to gasp aloud from the contact.

Bringing my hand back, I stick to my side of the tray to avoid further incident. Conversation carries on around me but my mind strays to last night and the way Silas kissed me. The way he touched me. My body is getting hot just from thinking about it. If I don't stop, the others will surely notice the flush I can feel creeping up.

A bump to the toe of my skate has me looking up from the tray of nachos. Silas is staring at me with a grin a mile wide. Amusement shines in his eyes and I know he can tell where my mind went just now.

Hours later, the four of us exit the building. Ronnie takes my hand in his as we reach Amy's car. "Monika, I'd love to see you again."

Oh, did he think tonight was a date? I didn't even know he would be here, Amy never said anything. Probably because she knew I would say no. "Oh, um, yeah, maybe."

He beams at me, leaning in and kissing my cheek. "Great. I'll get your number from Amy and call you."

Beside me, I can practically feel the anger rolling off Silas. Which is stupid since we agreed not to pursue each other. Ronnie whistles on his way to his truck. I groan and Amy claps in excitement. "I'm so glad you two got to meet. I know you think you're not ready to date, but he'll be good for you. Trust me. Much better than that grumpy asshole you were seeing."

My friend has no clue the extent of Brandon's grumpiness.

That man has a second personality that not many get to see. How lucky am I to have met that second personality? Not. My stomach rolls just thinking about him. "I don't think I'm ready to take that leap."

Laughter bubbles out of Amy. "Why not? That man is sexy as sin, he's kind, and he can cook. What's not to like?"

"Sis, leave her alone." Silas briefly glances in the direction Ronnie went. "If she doesn't want to date, then she doesn't want to date."

Amy waves him off. "I just want to see her happy. If you weren't my brother, then I might suggest you." Disgust wrinkles her nose. "First off, eww. And second, that's a big girl code violation."

Silas raises an eyebrow but says nothing.

Not paying her brother any mind, she shivers at the thought of the two of us together. "Friends don't sleep with their friend's brother. Period."

Ouch, that hit me square in the stomach. A quick peek at Silas and I see his lips form a tight line. We crossed a line last night. Stepping back from the two of them, I say, "We should get going." I don't get more than a step toward the passenger side when meowing catches my attention. It's not just a meow, but a distressed cry for help. "What's that?"

Silas and Amy quit talking and listen as well. "Is that a kitten?" Amy asks.

"Yes." Silas cranes his neck, listening to determine its location.

On the next cry, he and I both run toward the bushes at the far end of the parking lot. No cars are parked out in that area this time of the evening. As we approach, the beady eyes of the culprit stick out from the leaves. The light from the streetlamp turning them a wicked shade of red.

Unease sweeps over me at the vicious way the possum is staring at me, bloody drool dripping from his mouth. A mouth showcasing extremely sharp teeth. Teeth I imagine want to sink right into my flesh.

Silas surveys the area, presumably looking for an object to fight off the rabid looking possum. Amy unzips her purse and pulls out a small can of mace. With a shrill cry, she rushes forward, can aimed at the critter, and sprays.

The spray hits it mark and lands directly on the face of the possum. It hisses, more saliva dripping from its scary looking mouth. Silas comes up next to his sister, throwing a large rock that he found somewhere near the flowerbed by the building. When that rock hits the possum, it runs off, hissing. Concern for the kitten has me dashing forward, searching for the baby in distress.

Deep in the bushes is a small kitten, maybe nine or ten weeks old. Cream colored fur with streaks of charcoal gray in the face. The poor baby is shaking violently, so I approach slowly, as not to scare her further. My best friend and her brother stay back and keep silent while I attempt to get to the kitten.

Kneeling into the dirt, I coo at the baby, hoping to calm her nerves. It must work because she doesn't fight me or run away when I reach out for her. As soon as I gather her in my arms and get her into the light, I gasp at what I see.

TWELVE
Silas

Unsure of what is hiding in the bushes, I wait at the edge with my sister, holding her arm to keep her from marching forward and upsetting the animal. I know my sister well and I can tell by the way her body twitches that she is itching to rush forward and help Monika with the kitten.

When Monika gasps, I take a tentative step forward, gesturing at Amy to stay put. Monika makes shushing noises and is gently petting the kitten on the head. The little guy looks like he might be ten weeks, give or take. As Monika steps fully into the light, I see what had her gasping.

Red coats the end of his tail but that's not what concerns me. What has me concerned is the fact half of his tail is missing. As in that possum chewed it off. Giving a nod toward my car, I say a goodbye to my sister. "Amy, I'll see you tomorrow." To Monika, I say, "Hope in, we need to get him to the clinic."

Clutching the little guy to her chest, she slides into the passenger seat the minute I open the door. So, she doesn't have to jostle him around, I lean in and fasten the seatbelt around her. Since I keep my gym bag in the trunk, I pop it open and dig my towel out of the bag and hand it to her when I enter the car. She wraps it around the kitten, speaking in hushed tones. His ears perk up as he listens to every word coming from her mouth.

I've never seen a stray animal as content as this one is with her.

The trip back to Morris is quick and the entire ride Monika soothes the baby in her arms. I park as close to the front door as I can and rush to her side to open the passenger side door. Then I unbuckle the seatbelt and grab her elbow to help her out of the car.

Inside the clinic it's pitch black, and I feel along the wall until my hand glides over the light switch, flipping it on. Monika, being familiar with the layout of the building, is halfway to the exam room by the time the lights illuminate the corridor. I jog to catch up with her so I can open the door.

Once we're inside, she lays him on the exam table, petting his long, thick fur. Now that we have him under bright lights, I can see that he has several injuries. I also note that he is indeed a male. One front paw has puncture wounds from a bite. Blood pools above his right eye where a laceration splits the flesh. Then there is the missing end of his tail.

While she has him distracted and held down, I draw blood and examine him further. I don't notice any other wounds but want to do an X-ray to make sure there isn't any other injuries that might require immediate attention.

To my surprise, he remains still while I run the machine. It takes several minutes to get the pictures, but once they're ready I pull them up on the monitor so we can examine them together. Other than damage to the bone in the front paw, this little guy looks good internally.

I give Monika the okay to get a soft food pouch and feed the kitten while I clean up his tail and tend to the other wounds. He purrs while he eats, slurping the food up faster than I can work. Which is fine because Monika thought ahead and brought several food pouches with her, as well as a bottle of water and a small bowl.

By the time I'm done cleaning all his wounds, other than the front paw, he is full and sleepy. We give him a mild sedative so we can tend to his paw. He sleeps while we work. Monika continues to comfort him with touch even though he is out like a light. And this, ladies and gentlemen, is what makes her the best this clinic has to offer. Her loving spirit, along with her medical knowledge, is why she's the greatest technician I've had the pleasure to work with.

I leave her to bandage him up while I head to the office to start his chart. Typing up all the notes takes no time at all. Then I open the browser and post a listing on LostPaws. Since he is so young and we found him at the skating rink outside of the neighborhood, I doubt he belongs to anyone. Most likely, he is just a stray that got separated from his momma.

A knock on the office door jars me from my thoughts. Monika steps in, wringing her hands in front of her. She worries her bottom lip like she's afraid to ask whatever is on her mind. I'm about to tell her to spit it out when she releases the lip with a pop. "I was hoping I could take the little one home to keep an eye on him. It's doubtful he has a family, but I'll return him if they do show up. I just don't want him to be alone."

And that is why she belongs in this line of work. She loves these animals fiercely and treats them no differently than she would a human under her care. Since tomorrow is Sunday and the clinic will be closed, I want him under my care for observation. "Negative."

"What?" Sadness washes over her face and I suspect that she has already fallen in love with the little furball. "Why? Surely you don't want to just leave him here overnight?"

"Of course not." Pushing back from my desk, I stand and point to the cabinet on the far wall. "What I'm saying, is that since I have all the necessary medical supplies at home, he should stay with me." I don't dare mention that suggesting he come home with me is a way to get her back into my personal space. Because I suspect she will want to go where he goes. Admittingly, I did get jealous tonight seeing her with that Ronnie guy.

"Oh, yeah, that makes sense." She walks to the cabinet I

gestured to and retrieves a cat carrier. "But don't think for one minute that I'm going to allow you to hog my baby boy." There she is, my fiery blonde beauty. I hated seeing her light fizzle out after her run in with her ex.

Speaking of, I need to contact my cousin down at the police department and get some advice on how to get that asshole locked up for abuse. I know he'll tell me that it's up to Monika and her pressing charges, but I can't stand by and do nothing.

Trying to appear as nonchalant as possible, I shrug my shoulders and take the cat carrier from her. "Feel free to come over and babysit so I can get my beauty rest."

Rolling her eyes, she walks out of the office. "Silas, you're so stupid."

I don't even bother hiding the smirk on my face. This back-and-forth banter is what I live for. Especially with her. Reminds me of our younger years. She was feisty back then as well. Back then it made me want to wrap her in my protection. Now, I want to wrap her in my arms for a lot more than protection.

On cue, my eyes travel down to her round ass, watching as it sways left and right. I find myself wanting to reach out and grab it, throwing her against the wall, and doing filthy things to her.

The zipper on my jeans suddenly feels too tight. If I don't stop with this line of thinking, I will end up breaking the vow I made just this morning. After hearing my sister say *friends don't sleep with their best friend's brother,* I know I can't kiss her again. That would ruin their friendship.

Sometimes being the responsible older brother sucks donkey balls.

Careful not to jostle his injured paw, Monika scoops up the ragdoll kitten and places him inside the carrier. "All set." She slings her purse over her shoulder. "Guess I'm spending the night with you."

"Try to keep your hands off me this time," I joke.

"You hear that?" she asks the kitten. "Doctor McKade thinks

he's funny." Her eyes gaze in my direction. "But we know the truth, don't we baby?"

Not bothering with a reply, I lead the way out the door, locking the clinic behind us. I'm not the least bit surprised that she is refusing to put the carrier in the backseat. Instead, she wants him on her lap so she can see him.

When we get to my place, I show her to the guest bedroom and help her set up a place for the kitten. In the garage are a few boxes I had used when I moved. I find one big enough for the animal and bring it into the room for her.

She folds one of the baby blankets that we keep at the clinic and places it in the box. Then she scoops up her still sleeping furball and settles him in his new bed. "There you go, Luca."

"Luca?" Since when did she decide to give him a name?

"Well, I'm certainly not going to keep calling him kitten." She blows out a puff of air. "He deserves a name, so I gave him one."

"I see."

Resting her hands on her hips, she raises an eyebrow. "Besides, if no one claims him, I'm keeping him."

I take a step toward her. "And what if I want to keep him?"

Laughing, she shakes her head. Then she stops and freezes. "Oh, you're serious?"

Smiling, I say, "As a heart attack."

Stepping to the side, she blocks the path to the box where Luca rests. "Uh, no. I found him, I'm keeping him."

Tapping the end of her nose, I give her wink. "We'll work out custody arrangements later. Right now, I'm off to bed."

Never in a million years did I think I would add an animal to my homelife. Do I love them? Yes, you have to be an animal lover to be a veterinarian. But to have one as a pet, it was never in my plans. Now look at me. One night with Monika and I'm willing to adopt a pet just to keep her in my personal life.

When did I become this domesticated? And for what? For a woman that I cannot have, but desperately want.

Setting a bag on the dresser, I pull out a few small cans of soft cat food that I gathered from the clinic. "I don't have a pet dish, but feel free to grab a saucer and bowl from the kitchen."

"Okay, thanks." Glancing around, her shoulders slump and I worry I've said or done something wrong. Before I can ask what's bothering her, she asks a question. "Would you mind loaning me a shirt to sleep in?"

THIRTEEN
Monika

Sun shines through the open curtain, forcing my eyes open. I groan because I feel like I haven't slept in weeks. Sitting up, I rub the sleep from my eyes and lean over to peek into the box. Shoving the blanket from my body, I jump out of bed and drop to my knees to peer under the bed.

There is no sign of the kitten anywhere. "Luca?" I search the room, checking the closet and en suite bathroom. "Here kitty, kitty."

Panic sets in and I frantically search every drawer of the dresser, behind the curtain, and inside the bathroom trashcan. Silly, I know. When I don't find him anywhere, I dash out of the room. Silas is standing in the kitchen flipping pancakes. He turns around at the sound of my footsteps. "Hey, good morning." His eyes rake over my body, lingering on my bare legs, but I'm too concerned for Luca to pay attention to the heat darkening the gray of his irises.

"Have you seen Luca? I can't find him anywhere." That's when I hear it. The smacking sound of a kitten eating soft food. I step around the island and see him perched on a mat, his tiny face inside a bowl as he devours the food Silas set out for him.

Platting the pancake, he smiles down at Luca. "I heard him crying and figured he was hungry." With a smirk, he adds, "Or it could have been your snoring that woke him."

Oh, my goodness, do I snore? Surely not. Did I snore when I slept in his bed that night? Now I'm mortified. Wondering what he might think of me. Earth swallow me whole. There's nothing to be done about it now. "Whatever, I do not snore. If anything, your snoring shook the whole house and woke him."

"Don't be jealous now." He cast a glance over his shoulder. "We both know I sleep like a king and don't make a sound."

I roll my eyes and drop the subject of me snoring. Instead, I pick up Luca after he polishes off the last of his food. "How's my good boy?" Immediately, he begins purring, rubbing his head under my chin.

When Silas carries the plates to the table, I can't help but stare at the man. He sits at the table without a shirt, all those muscles rippling with each move he makes. I watch as he piles two pancakes, several strips of bacon, a heaping serving of eggs, and three sausage patties onto his plate.

That is a lot of food, and I can't help but balk at the number of calories he is piling up. Days like today, when the sweet aroma permeates the air, I wish I could eat food like that. But I can't. I'm one of those people that smell food and gain weight. Which is why Brandon always asked me to eat in the other room when he brought home takeout. He said I couldn't afford to inhale the calories.

Kissing my sweet boy between his ears, I take him back to the bedroom. The two of us sit on the bed, him in my arms purring up a storm, and me, avoiding the scent of pancakes with maple syrup. Gah, my stomach growls just thinking about it.

"You know, Luca, I hope no one claims you. For real." I rub the spot between his eyes, smoothing his fur back. "Do you know why?" He blinks up at me like he can understand every word coming from my mouth. "I want you all to myself."

We cuddle and I sing to him, until there's a knock on the door. I yell for Silas to enter, and he pushes the door open. "Hey, the food is getting cold."

"Oh." I didn't realize he was waiting for me to start eating. "Go ahead and eat."

Leaning against the doorframe, he crosses his muscular arms over his chest. "What about you?" His express turns serious. No nonsense. "And I don't want to hear any bullshit about not being hungry."

"Okay." A part of me wants to join him at the dining room table, but the other part, the much bigger part refuses. "Um, can you just bring me a single serving of eggs? Please."

"You want to eat in here?" He looks about the room, then back at me. I nod. "That's not how we do things around here." Pushing from the doorframe, he takes the kitten from my arms and places him back in his box. "Come on."

Lowering my head, I say, "I can't."

"Why the hell not?" When I flinch at his stern tone, he softens his voice. With a finger to my chin, he tilts my head until I'm forced to look at him. "Why?"

I'm too ashamed to admit it. To say what he can plainly see on my body. Why was I cursed with this chunky physique? The body my mom always called big boned. Silas pinches my chin, reminding me that he asked a question and wants an answer. "Because you made pancakes."

Shock widens his eyes. "Do they stink? I thought they smelled delicious."

"No, it's not that." My nose starts to burn signaling the beginning of tears. Inhaling a deep breath, I pray they recede. I've cried enough in front of this man.

"Okay, then." Dropping my chin, he takes my hand, hauling me to my feet. "Let's go eat some breakfast."

Digging my heals into the floor, I resist his pull. "Silas, no, I can't. Please just bring me some eggs. I promise to eat them."

"Unless you can provide me with a valid reason, the answer is no." He still has ahold of my hand. "In this house, we eat at the table. Together."

Great, this is the most mortifying situation ever. "It's okay,

I'm not even that hungry." To prove me a liar, my stomach grumbles loud enough for the whole neighborhood to hear.

"Is that so?" He points at my belly. "Because your stomach says otherwise. How about you drop the bullshit and come eat."

Tired of this back and forth that is going nowhere, I cave. He may look at me differently after this. *Or,* the voice in the back of my mind says, *he may be understanding like he has shown prior.* "I can't eat in there with the pancakes and maple syrup, I'll gain ten pounds just from smelling it."

Silas bursts out laughing, but when he sees that I haven't joined in, he stops. "You're serious?" His irises darken with anger. "Is that what Brandon told you?" My silence says it all. "You know that's not true at all, don't you? You cannot gain weight by being in the same room as food."

In my heart I know that to be true, but my mind is a mess.

Tipping my chin up, Silas smooths his thumb across my bottom lip. His eyes tracking the movement. "Brandon is an abuser. Everything he has ever said to you has been a lie. Guys like him build themselves up by tearing others down."

Again, this is all stuff I know deep down, but my head and heart are at war.

No nonsense Silas is back, and he doesn't accept no as answer. "Come out of this room and join me for breakfast." How does he do it? Get me to overcome insecurities with just a simple command.

I follow him to the dining room and sit across from him. Silas reheats the food then sets a plate of eggs and fruit in front of me. The serving is bigger than what I would have given myself, but that seems to be the way Silas does things.

The serving on his plate is massive and I have to admit, watching him cut up his pancake and sausage, and mixing it with bacon and egg then shoveling it in his mouth makes me want to do the same. His eyes track the movement of my tongue as it glides over my lips. "You want a bite, sweetheart?"

Yes. "No."

With a smirk, he forks another mixture. "Liar." Then he leans across the table, holding it to my lips. When I don't immediately open, he coaxes my lips apart with the food. "Eat."

My will is battling with my fears, but when he makes that simple demand, I open wide and accept the food he offers. Never in a million years would I pile sausage, bacon, and eggs on my pancake and drizzle it with syrup. It just doesn't look like it belongs together, but the second those flavors hit my tongue its pure heaven.

Smiling in satisfaction, he points to the stack of pancakes in the center of the table. "Would you like some?"

"Oh, no thank you." Picking up a strawberry, I focus on the fruit. Amy always said I was weird because I eat my fruit before the hot food. Weird or not, that's me. I enjoy the sweet stuff first.

Between bites, I watch him though my lashes. I think I'm being sneaky but then he scoots his chair next to mine. Once I've polished off the fruit, he forks another bite and holds it to my lips. This time I don't argue, it's pointless anyway. Silas has a way of getting what he wants, and he seems hellbent on feeding me.

Without realizing it, I've eaten half of the food on his plate. Glancing at my own, I see there is a small portion of my eggs left. While talking with Silas, I have eaten more carbohydrates than I would in a week. Hell, more than I would eat in a month. I want to hate myself and force the contents back up my throat, but the way his gray orbs shine with something akin to pride washes away the guilt and shame.

Silas makes me feel a certain way, a way I haven't felt in ten years. He makes me feel safe, accepted, and free. For the first time in three years, I ate carbohydrates and sugars. Ate them freely without fretting over every single bite.

There is still a pancake leftover and while I stack the dishes to carry to the kitchen, Silas picks it up and stuffs it in his mouth. He is right behind me with the last plate. "I can take care of the dishes, why don't you check in on the baby."

As stupid as it sounds, those words make me feel like we're a family. If only for a little while. It's like the two of us are playing house. God, I'm a huge dummy for thinking such a thing, I know. But a girl can dream, right?

FOURTEEN
Silas

Two days. Two days of Monika living at my house. She refuses to leave Luca in my care. Absurd considering my profession. Her scent lingers everywhere. On the sofa, in the hallway. Hell, she's even replaced my regular coffee with her blueberry flavored java. Though, I'll admit, I'm beginning to acquire a taste for the odd flavor.

Today is a slow day at the clinic and Monika has Luca out, showing him off to the staff. Everyone is oohing and awing over the furry feline. When she finally decides to settle down and start a family, I have a feeling she will be a great mom. If her actions with the kitten are anything to go by.

Where that thought came from, I don't know.

Since the day is mostly vaccinations and checkups, I leave that to Monika. She has Jose as an assistant and the two of them work well together. I need to keep distance between us because I'm finding it harder and harder to resist her. Which makes it damn near impossible to stick to my hands off rule.

While I'm regarding the file for tomorrow's surgery, my sister sends a text.

> Amy: Want to go out tonight? Andromeda?
> I'm thinking of inviting Ronnie so he and Monika can get to know each other.

Just the mention of his name irks my nerves. Monika deserves so much more than that guy. At least that's what I tell myself. The truth is, I want Monika and the thought of her with another man sends me into a fit of jealousy.

> Silas: Not tonight. We have Luca and he needs lots of medical attention right now.

That's not the whole truth. Yes, he does need us to clean his tail wound, as well as his injured paw, but he doesn't need constant care like I'm suggesting. She doesn't need to know that though. This is just a means of getting her to hold off on getting those two together. I need her to hold off on hooking them up for my own sanity.

> Amy: That's right. She's been staying at your place to help with his care.

Though that's the truth, Monika has been staying at my house to help with Luca's care, we have also been getting to know each other. At night we sit up watching television, chatting about anything and everything. She is even coming around where food is concerned. The last two days she has eaten more than a measly bite of protein. It took a bit of a push on my part —okay, it took me being demanding and not taking no for an answer—but seeing her enjoy the foods she was denying herself is priceless.

> Amy: Okay, some other time then.

Thank the good Lord.

> Silas: Yes, another day. Maybe in a week or two.

Luca doesn't need that long, but I won't tell her that. I selfishly want Monika all to myself. For as long as I can have her.

At the end of the day, I do a walk through to make sure the

clinic is tidy and sterilized. Most everyone has left for the day, all that remains is Monika and Jose. I find them in the back, spraying down the kennels and taking out the trash. Luca is already in his cat carrier, ready to go.

After locking the backdoor, Jose waves. "Good night, I'll see you guys in the morning."

"Night," Monika and I say in unison.

Picking up the carrier, I follow Monika out the front door, shutting off lights as we go. She rubs her eyes with the back of her hands, yawning as she opens the passenger side door. "How about we grab some dinner on the way home? I don't think either of us feel like cooking tonight."

"Right you are." She buckles her seatbelt, tucks the carrier between her feet, and leans back, closing her eyes.

It appears she is worn out. I wonder if Luca kept her awake last night. Maybe I should offer to keep him in my room tonight. On the way home, well technically not on the way since I have to drive out to Okmulgee for food, I stop by Just My Slice and pick up a large pizza, wings, and a salad because I know Monika will want to fill up on the rabbit food before consuming the pepperoni pie.

She is sound asleep when I pull into the drive, so I set the food on the hood of the car and open the passenger door to shake her awake. Grunting, she turns her head and twists as much as the seatbelt will allow.

Chuckling, I unbuckle the belt and shake her again. "Come on, Monika, we're home." She makes an unintelligible noise. "Hey, wake up. I have dinner."

"No thanks." She waves me off.

Needing her to get out of the car, I say the one thing I hope will bring her to her senses. "Luca needs to get inside so he can stretch out." That seems to do the trick.

Monika opens her eyes and glances down at her fur baby. "Alright sweet boy, it's time to get you fed."

I highly doubt that cat needs to eat. Pretty sure he has eaten all day long. Some soft food here, a snack there. Regardless, I'll sit back and watch her spoil the kitten. It makes her happy, and what makes her happy, makes me happy.

Seems I'm turning into a sap.

As expected, Monika feeds the cat before tending to her own needs. Because my momma raised me to respect those around me, I sit at the table waiting for her to join me. When she finally comes in and notices the unopened boxes, shame washes over her. "Silas, you do not have to wait for me."

"Nonsense." Passing a plate to her, I wait for her to get her fill before digging in. Over the past couple of days, I have been working hard to get her to eat more, and tonight she fills the plate with mostly salad, but there is a slice of pizza and four wings. This is a major improvement from the girl she was a week ago.

We talk and laugh, enjoying the food and the company. Since I bought a large pizza, there is plenty for leftovers. Which I will take to work for my lunch tomorrow. She stands and stretches. "I'm off to shower and then I'm going straight to bed, I'm beat."

Taking the plate from her, I nod. "See you in the morning." Just as she reaches the hallway, I remember the cat. "I'm taking Luca to my room tonight."

Spinning on her heel, she marches back into the kitchen. "Why?"

Tossing the leftover pizza into a Ziplock bag, I place it in the fridge and then address her question. "So, I can take care of him." Honestly, he doesn't need us fusing over him. He is healing nicely and doing well on his own.

Hands on her hips, she looks offended. "Are you trying to say that I'm a bad cat mom?"

It sounds absurd and I laugh. "No, Monika, I'm saying you need to share him with his dad." How the hell did I turn into a cat dad. "Now, go take your shower and get some rest."

"Jeez, you're so bossy."

Yes, I am. "That's why they call me the boss."

"You are seriously so dumb." She laughs at her own joke then heads to her room.

Since we ate takeout, the clean-up is fast. She's still in the shower when I enter her room to get Luca. He grunts when I lift his box. Very few cats I've tended to over the years were grunters. It's not a painful grunt, just a general *you're disturbing me* grunt. "You're okay."

My room is at the end of the hall so I'm not far if Monika wants to poke her head in and check on Luca. I set his box under the window. It's a clear view from the bed, so I will be able to see him from where I lay.

I don't expect her to check on him any time soon, so I close my bedroom door and head to the shower. Monika is good about not entering my room when I have it closed. Leaving the bathroom door open just a crack, I turn on the water and wait for it to warm.

Connecting to the Bluetooth speaker, I hit play on my playlist and strip down. The water is hot, just the way I like it. Showering is relaxing and I adjust the showerhead to Jetstream so it can beat the knots out of my shoulders. I should look into finding a good chiropractor to help with those stress knots. Regular alignments would do me a world of good.

Humming at the pleasant feel of the water, I find myself recounting the last week. How my life has changed drastically during this time. Pining for the forbidden fruit. Co-parenting a cat. Who knew that was a thing? I damn sure didn't. Although, I've never owned a pet before. Shocking, I know considering I take care of them for a living.

Here I am, taking on the role of cat dad, and enjoying it.

By the time two songs play through, I'm done washing. Grabbing the towel from the hook, I step out of the shower and dry off. *You Should Probably Leave* is the next song to play and I find myself singing along, momentarily forgetting about the blonde just a couple doors down. I'm lost to the song and don't register the soft click of a door in the other room.

As the song nears the end, I hang the towel and push open the bathroom door. My focus is on my cell phone and the email app I have open. So, in all my naked glory, I walk to the dresser for a change of underwear. Then I happen to look in the mirror and see a pair of blue deer-in-headlights eyes staring at me. More accurately, at my ass cheeks.

FIFTEEN
Monika

Slipping into my Ghostface nightgown, I stare at the empty corner where Luca has slept the last couple of nights. Sadness tugs at my heart and I find myself wandering down the hall toward Silas's bedroom. Rapping my knuckles on the door, I wait for the green light to enter.

There is no response, so I knock again. "Silas?" Faint sounds of music filter through the door, followed by his voice as he sings along. Turning the knob, I crack the door and call out again. "Silas?"

He doesn't answer, but I don't hear the shower running so I ease the door open further. I can hear him in the bathroom singing and judging by the footwork, he's also dancing. Cool. While he performs for his invisible audience, I will say goodnight to Luca.

Silas and I have been keeping an eye on our post in LostPaws. So far no one has claimed him as their missing baby. Several have commented on how beautiful he is. How fluffy his cream-colored fur is and how blue his eyes are. The plan is to wait until the beginning of next week before we go through with his adoption. Or rather, before I sign the paperwork for his adoption. I'll be damned if I share custody of a cat.

Squatting, I run the tip of my finger from the base of his nose, back between his ears. He grunts, which I'm finding he does a lot. Then his little motor starts up and he purrs loudly, shifting his body so I can reach his belly. Very trusting for a stray.

A squeak of the door has me glancing up from where I'm squatting. With his nose in his cell phone, he doesn't see me. Has no idea that he has an intruder invading his personal space. I should say something, anything, but I don't. I'm frozen to the spot, my gaze on his dick as it swings with his movements.

As his back turns to me, I can't help but stare at his ass as it flexes with each step toward the dresser. Oh. My. God. I should look away. Close my eyes. Make a noise. Anything to gain his attention. I know this wrong, spying on him, but I can't find it in myself to care. Seeing him in all his glory stirs the lust that is always lingering under the surface.

I've had a taste of him once, and I want another.

Heaven help me, I want him. To hell with the consequences.

His hand is halfway to the dresser drawer when his body suddenly goes rigid. I don't need to see his face to know he's spotted me spying on him from my crouched position by the window. It's evident in the stiffness of his posture. Which does wicked things to his gluts. Those muscles flex, leaving a dimple in the side of his ass cheek. A dimple I desperately want to run my tongue over.

"Monika?"

"Hum?" Proper words fail to form and all I can manage is a quiet hum.

His body relaxes and he turns around to face me, though that only serves to bring his dick back into my line of sight. "Hey." Silas snaps his fingers. "My eyes are up here." I suck my bottom lip into my mouth and bite down to prevent a moan from escaping. When our gazes lock, he smirks. "Good girl."

Keeping my eyes on his, I crawl toward him, putting extra sway in my hips. Only Silas can command my body without saying a word. His nostrils flare when he inhales. Those gray eyes darkening as he tracks my movements.

Stopping at his feet, I sit back on mine. I'm not sure if it's the fact I'm on my knees, but his once limp dick has hardened and is now standing at attention. Leaning forward, I kiss the base of him, licking up the length. I've never done this before, so I'm not quite sure how to suck a guy off. All I know is what I've seen from Brandon's porno videos. Hopefully, I don't make a fool of myself.

Groaning, he threads his fingers through my hair and grips a fistful. "Monika, what are you doing?" When I open my mouth and suck him to the back of my throat, he moans. "You were the one quick to end our sexcapades."

The way he moans and jerks in my mouth lets me know that I'm doing something right. Otherwise, he wouldn't respond this way. Would he? No, I don't believe so. This gives me hope that I can please him like he did me our first night together.

It may have been me that spoke first that morning to end this before it started, but we both know he was thinking the same thing. I just beat him to the punch. Releasing him with a pop, I sit back on my feet. "You want me to stop?"

Eyes wide like he's afraid I will leave him like this, he shakes his head. "Hell no." He guides me back to his length. "You started this. You're going to finish it." It comes out as a demand, but I know he would stop if I had second thoughts. Silas is not the type of man to force a woman into giving him pleasure. He is not Brandon.

Opening my mouth, I take him in and bob my head. I don't have to worry if I'm doing a good job because Silas is very vocal, moaning and praising. The number of times he says *good girl* and *that's it, sweetheart, you're doing so good* is more than I can count. Hearing that stirs butterflies in my belly, sending shockwaves straight to my clit. Who knew I had a praise kink? Assuming that's what this is called. Hell if I know.

The more unraveled he gets, the more turned on I get. Sensations build in my core, turning my insides to lava. My abdomen quivers with the building tenson. I moan around him, and his fist tightens in my hair, stinging my scalp. It's not so painful it hurts, but it's just painful enough to add to my pleasure.

"Damn, sweetheart, you feel so good." He throws his head back, pumping his hips ever so slowly. With a hiss, he releases my hair and pulls back. "Much more of that and I'll come down your throat." Hauling me to my feet, he says, "And that's not how I want this night to end."

Cupping my face, he kisses me slow and sweet. His tongue probs inside my mouth, dominating yet sensual. I'm not sure how we will break this to his sister, but for the life of me, I can't stay away from him. My body craves his touch. Like I may not survive without it. He is like oxygen to my deprived lungs.

Wrapping my arms around his neck, I mold my body to his. I need to be close to him. The need to have him inside me is overwhelming. Is it possible to combust from pent-up sexual need?

Unable to wait a second longer, I break the kiss and flip off the light. With the lights out, I pull the nightgown over my head, tossing it on the dresser. Standing before him in nothing but my lacey panties, I reach out to grab his hand, but he moves it away. To my horror, he flips the light switch, revealing me in all my glory. Or not so glory.

Shame rears its ugly head and I lift my hands to hide my breasts. Unlike my ex, Silas smiles warmly as he pries my hands away. "There is nothing to be ashamed of. Your body is sexy just the way it is." Kissing the tip of my nose, he leans his forehead against mine. "I will tell you how beautiful you are until you believe it. I will show you how desirable you are, until you feel it in your bones."

Just like that, my fears start to fade and desire for this man comes back full force. This time I don't worry or flinch when he hooks his thumbs in my panties and shoves them down. I kick the fabric to the side and let him guide me backward.

When the backs of my legs hit the mattress, Silas lifts me off the ground, laying me in the center of the bed. He spreads my legs wide, exposing my dripping core. "Look how wet you are for me." Diving in, he licks from my opening to my clit, paying special attention to the sensitive nub.

Working him over with my mouth already had me on the edge, so it doesn't take long for him to get me off. Toes curling and back arching, I let out a cry as I fist his hair, holding him in place. He places tiny kisses on my tender flesh as I come down from my orgasm. When I release his hair, he moves away from the bed to get a condom from his bedside table.

Tearing the foil with his teeth, he slides the latex down his length and motions for me to slide to the edge of the bed. The moment I'm at the edge, he pulls me up and spins me around, bending me over the mattress.

With one hand, he grips both of my wrists, pinning them above my head. "This body was made for pleasure. Yours and mine." Then he aligns himself with my entrance and sinks in. We both moan at the sensation.

His hips move painfully slow, and his free hand finds my breast, rubbing across the hardened nipple. Every inch of my body is on fire, and I know it won't be long before I detonate again. He must feel it too because he pumps faster, pinching harder, until I shatter around him. Squeezing him with my inner walls.

Letting go of my wrists, his hands grip my hips, squeezing, and his thrusts come faster. There is no rhythm to his movements anymore. "Yes." His head falls to the spot between my shoulder blades. "That's my good girl."

I didn't think it was possible, but those last four words set off another orgasm, more powerful than the last.

Gripping my jaw, he turns my head so he can kiss me. "You like that?" His eyes bore into mine. "You like when I talk to you like that?"

My body is on overload and my brain forgets how to form words. So, I nod and manage to say, "Uh huh." I love it when he praises me during sex. He is the first man who has ever spoken praise to me. Granted, he is the only man outside of my ex I've been with.

"Good." Crashing his lips to mine, he devours me with his kiss.

If there was a dream I never wanted to wake from, this would be it. Silas is every fantasy come to life. He's demanding, yet gentle. Wild and rough, yet soft and sweet. Frantically pumping into me, he sucks my tongue in his mouth. How I wish I could turn around and wrap my legs around his waist.

Releasing my tongue, he says, "Your body is amazing." With a final thrust, his body stills. His weight leaning into mine. Not to the point I'm uncomfortable. When he starts to soften, he pulls out.

Tossing the used condom in the trash, he fetches a wet rag and cleans me. Just like he did the last time. It may be a small gesture, but it means more to me than he will ever know. The action makes me feel well cared for.

When I head toward the door, he takes hold of my hand. "Where are you going?"

"To my room." I figured that since he got what he needed that he wouldn't want me sleeping in his bed. Yes, the last time I slept in his bed, but that was different. I was a guest and invited into his personal space. This time I have my own room. Albeit a temporary room.

"Stay." He doesn't say another word, just pleads with his eyes.

Leaving my nightgown where it is, I crawl back into his bed and lay my head on his shoulder. Breathing in his masculine scent.

SIXTEEN
Silas

Life with Monika is starting to feel more and more like a relationship. She is the last thing I see at night, and the first I see in the morning. We eat breakfast together, ride to work together, shower together. Showering with her is so much more enjoyable than showering alone.

We haven't discussed labels. Hell, we haven't discussed my sister and how this will affect her. For the time being, we are a couple behind closed doors and colleagues out in the open. Amy has texted Monika several times, trying to get her to go out with her friend Ronnie. Each time, Monika has replied that she is busy with Luca. Thank God, because my sanity would be on the line otherwise.

I know it's a matter of time before Amy decides to force Monika out kicking and screaming. That's just how my sister rolls. Let's hope it doesn't come to that. Because then I would be forced to spill our truth to my sister, and finding out like that would set her off in the worst way.

At work, a couple of people have raised an eyebrow at us arriving together. Luckily, no one has mentioned it to either of us. Most likely because they see me as the hard ass boss that I try so hard to be while in the office. In front of colleagues, Monika and I carry on as we always have. Only now we have Luca. Which Monika insists we bring him to work each day.

She's even set up a cat tower in the back room for him to

lounge on. Everyone adores him, he's become the clinic kitten. He has more toys than any animal should have, all thanks to the staff. Luca is the king of this castle, AKA the clinic, and he's not afraid to show it. That furball struts around like he owns the place, demanding attention and treats.

Tonight, Monika and I are curled up on the sofa, watching an episode of *Real Life in the ER*. It's not my cup of tea but watching her is. Luca is currently lying on her lap, purring up a storm. His tail has healed nicely. It's short and stubby, and it puffs out to the size of my wrist with his thick fur.

As for his paw, the wounds have healed over. There are a few scabs still but otherwise it's looking good. Sensing my eyes on him, he lifts his head and leans toward my hand. Like with his momma, I can't help but to give in to his requests. Spoiled cat, that's what he is.

The sound of a key in the door has us jolting away from one another. Like teenagers being caught making out in the basement. Stupid, considering this is my house and I'm a grown ass man. I turn around when the front door opens, knowing it can only be one person.

Amy strolls in carrying two bags of takeout, the logo on the plastic is from the diner she works at. I stand up and take the bags from her, carrying them to the dining room table. When I turn back around, Ronnie is crossing the threshold. He makes a beeline for Monika, handing her a bouquet of roses.

What. The. Hell.

Monika turns her wide eyes in my direction. Apparently, she is as shocked as I am. What was my sister thinking? Not once did she call me and ask if she could bring a visitor to my house. If she had, I would have said no. Not just no, but hell no.

He better not expect her to bring those flowers in here and put them in a vase. For one, I don't own a vase. Two, I'd rather toss them in the garbage, where they belong. Don't get me wrong, Monika deserves flowers, just not from that jerkwad.

Amy waltzes into the kitchen, smiling a megawatt smile. "Don't they make the cutest couple?"

"No."

She ignores me and opens the cabinet to get plates. Noticing I haven't untied the bags, she takes them from me and lines the boxes on the island in neat rows. "Come eat, you two." My sister's singsong voice grates on my nerves tonight. I wish she would take her friend and leave. Or just send him on his way. In fact, that sounds like the best option. We don't need him here to enjoy this meal.

Ronnie stretches out his hand to Monika. She peeks over at me but takes his offered hand which only serves to anger me further. Monika is mine. Ronnie has no business touching her in any way, shape, or form. If looks could kill, that man would be dead already because my fury is aimed right at the asshole.

As if pulling it from thin air, Amy produces a vase. She runs water into it and then takes the roses from Monika, arranging them neatly and placing them in the center of the dining room table. If I didn't want to punch Ronnie before, I sure as hell do now.

Monika loads her plate with salad and sits in her usual spot. Not wanting my sister and Ronnie to take up the seats next to her, I quickly pile my plate high and rush to sit to her left. She smiles at me as she picks at her rabbit food.

Amy sits next to me, leaving the seat to the right of Monika open for Ronnie. "So, how is Luca healing?" Amy watches our kitten with interest. "He seems to be getting around really well."

Monika swallows the small amount of food before answering. "Yes, he is. There are still some wounds on his paw that are tender, but otherwise he's doing well."

There goes our freedom. Now that Amy knows Luca is doing fine, she will begin heavily pushing Ronnie and Monika together. I'm not sure how much of that I can take. I'm already exploding with jealousy. Without thinking about current company, I cut off a piece of my steak and slip it onto Monika's plate. If Amy notices, she's polite enough not to say anything. Ronnie, on the other hand, looks like he is ready to murder me.

The feeling is mutual, trust me.

As I knew she would, Monika cuts the tiniest piece off the steak. It has been a hassle to get her to eat more than her rabbit food, but we are making progress. Any progress is better than none. My sister watches her friend eat the food I slide onto her plate and lifts a brow in my direction.

So, Amy has noticed that her best friend barely eats. I make a mental note to sit down and have a discussion with her later.

Since I know Monika hates carbohydrates, I only spoon a small amount of mac n cheese onto her plate. She eyes the cheesy pasta with disdain but then she meets my eyes. For a minute, I think she is going to refuse, especially since we have company, and she knows I wouldn't push her in front of them. To my satisfaction, she forks two noodles.

My eyes are riveted to her mouth as she closes her lips over the metal utensil. Tracking the movement of her tongue as she licks the cheese coating her lips. I have never been so entranced by a woman like I am with her.

Under the cover of the table, I grab her thigh and squeeze. My body craves any amount of contact I can get. Right now, it's this. If it weren't for our guests, I would pull her onto my lap and kiss her breathless, then take her to my bedroom and strip her bare.

The only sign that my touch affects her are the goosebumps that pebble her flesh. A smile spreads on my face, knowing my touch does this to her. One simple touch to her leg and her body responds in an instant.

Ronnie, to my disappointment, is chatting her ear off. I don't care enough to pay attention to what he has to say, not when I see how she reacts to my subtle touch. My sole focus is strictly on Monika. The way she nods her head at something he says, or murmurs an *uh huh*, but I can tell she's not really listening to what he has to say either.

She glances back at her plate, but for a split second her eyes peek over at me. A devilish smirk tilts the corner of her mouth and there's a challenge in her eyes. My insides perk up a little at the fact she's playing this game with me right under our guest's noses.

With slow, deliberate movements, she forks more mac n cheese. She knows how much I enjoy watching her eat her favorite foods, the ones she has been denying herself for far too long. Closing her lips over the prongs, she graces me with a brief look then when the creamy pasta hits her tongue she moans. Not loud, but enough I can hear.

That sound does it for me, I'm growing hard right here at the table in front of my sister. Not what a man wants to happen. Thank God, the wooden table hides it from everyone. Everyone except Monika.

Speaking of, Monika is back to nodding at Ronnie while she eats. I tune out their conversation, or rather his one-sided conversation, and sit back and watch her eat. It seems like she is eating for my attention while pretending to listen to this poor sap.

Who knew that watching a woman eat could be such an erotic act? Or it could be the fact that Monika is silently obeying my unspoken command that is setting me off. Either way, I'm ready for my sister and her friend to leave so I can have my wicked way with her.

Inching my fingers up her thigh, I'm shocked when Monika spreads her legs enough for my wandering hand. My dining table isn't big enough to hide more than what is currently taking place beneath it, but I'll take what I can get. For now.

Gliding my fingers underneath the leg of her shorts, I continue until I reach her lace panties. While my wandering hand is busy touching Monika, I pick up a dinner roll. I need to keep up appearances, so my sister doesn't notice what's happening between me and her best friend.

The bread is soft, but not as soft as Monika's smooth flesh when I slip my finger beneath the band of her panties. Monika chokes on water, and she sets her glass down to cover her mouth with a napkin.

Amy leans forward with concern. "Are you okay?"

"I'm fine." Monika coughs again, motioning for my sister to stay seated. "It just went down the wrong pipe."

Ronnie takes her free hand, rubbing circles on it while asking if there's anything he can do. There's one thing he can do, he can pack up and leave, damnit. Reclining in my seat, I continue stroking her wet slit while munching on the dinner roll. A roll that I desperately wish was Monika. I could eat her all day, if you catch my drift.

"I'm fine, thank you." Monika pulls her hand free.

Ronnie seems a bit defeated, but he recovers quickly, smiling at her like a lovestruck puppy.

At this point, I'm only eating to keep busy. To keep from leaning over and kissing her in front of the one person that wields the power to ruin what we're currently building. What we're doing is wrong, but we both seem helpless to stop.

Oh, the secrets we keep.

SEVENTEEN
Monika

Oh. My. God. Amy could stand up at any moment and get a glimpse of what is happening under this table. Hell, all Ronnie has to do is lean over and he could see what Silas is doing to me. When did I become this person? The person that allows a man to touch her intimately while sitting in the presence of friends.

I am in so much trouble if Amy ever finds out about this secret we're keeping.

Ronnie tries to hold my hand again, but I avoid his touch by clasping onto my glass in-between bites. Anything to keep my hand busy. The last thing I need is for him to think we're a couple. We most certainly are not a couple, and we never will be. He might be a handsome man, but my heart would never desire him the way I do Silas. My heart belongs to one man, and one man only. It always has. Even when I was dating Brandon, Silas owned me heart and soul.

Panic starts to set in when Amy pushes her chair back. She cannot see what her brother is doing to me right under her nose. It would set fire to the rain. This night is about to go to hell in a handbasket if she peeks down at my lap. Everyone sitting at this table is about to have their lives changed, and not for the better.

If I lower my hand and try to pry Silas's fingers from my panties, it will raise suspicions. So, how do I keep my best friend from discovering my best kept secret?

Thankfully, I don't have to do anything. Silas discretely removes his hand in the nick of time. Shooting me a wink, he stands up and clears both of our plates. Leaving our guests none the wiser.

I swear, this man loves living on the edge. Has he always been this way? I may have a heart attack if this keeps happening.

Ronnie stands and holds his hand out to me. "Take a walk with me."

From across the room, I swear I hear a growl. As I stand, I glance back at Silas. If looks could kill, Ronnie would be a dead man walking. Now I feel like I'm stuck between a rock and a hard place. If I go outside with Ronnie, Silas will flip his lid. If I don't, I can't let him down gently. I need to have this conversation in private, away from Amy who is currently trying to push us together.

"I'll be back in a minute." Amy smiles at me, but Silas looks like he wants to punch Ronnie in the throat, and then toss me over his shoulder like a caveman. I try to gain his attention, to silently convey that everything is okay. That I'm not going out there to make out with this man who is basically a stranger. But his gaze is trained on Ronnie.

Bypassing his outstretched hand, I stand and motion for Ronnie to follow me outside. Disappointment crosses his face, but he is quick to school his features. Just not quick enough for me to not notice.

The sound of Amy putting away the leftovers follows us to the door. Before I can reach for the doorknob, Ronnie reaches around me and holds the door open for me. He is such a gentleman. I almost feel bad for the news I'm about to break to him.

Almost.

When the door closes behind us, I walk to the edge of the porch and lean my arms on the railing, looking out toward the road. His quiet footsteps follow. I don't know how to start this conversation. I've never had to let a guy down before.

Out of my peripheral, I see him mirror my position. A long-drawn-out sigh leaves his mouth, and we continue to stand in silence for a few minutes. It's awkward and I'm not sure what to do or how to act. I think I'd prefer to get hit by a truck at this point.

"You're not into me, are you?" Ronnie turns to face me.

I close my eyes, hoping I don't say something to upset him. Praying he understands and doesn't lash out at me like Brandon would in this situation. "I'm sorry."

A sad smile tips his lips. "It happens." Looking back at the house, then back to me, he asks, "Is there someone else that holds your interest?"

"No." I shake my head. When he lifts a brow, I let out a puff of air. "Well, maybe." Then remembering he is friends with Amy, I'm quick to add, "But I want to keep it quiet for now."

"Understood." Picking up my hand, Ronnie kisses the back of it. "I wish you the best, Monika." When the curtain pulls back, light spills out onto the porch. Turing around, I see Silas standing in the window with his arms crossed over his chest and a glare in his gaze. Ronnie releases my hand. He must put two and two together, because he whispers, "Your secret is safe with me. I promise."

Oh no, if Ronnie can put the pieces together, I'm sure Amy can as well. I can't have that. This needs to remain top secret until I figure out a way to break the news to her. After they leave, Silas and I need to have a chat about being discreet. Turning my back to Silas, I smile at Ronnie. "Thank you, and I'm truly sorry about us."

"Don't be." He gazes out toward the street. "Somewhere out there is a girl made just for me." Meeting my stare, he adds, "I won't settle for less, and neither should you."

Wow, where was this guy five years ago? I would have much rather dated him than Brandon. As I look back at Silas who is still hovering at the window, I'm glad things worked out the way they did, because it led me to the place that I'm at now. A place with Silas by my side, taking care of me. In more ways than one.

When we walk in, Amy is sitting on the sofa with Luca in her arms, cooing to him like he's a newborn baby. By the looks of it, my fur baby is eating up the extra attention. He is in full blown purr mode. That fluffy, stubby tail is swinging back and forth in glee.

Seeing me, she sets him on the cushion next to her and comes toward me, smiling. Don't smile, Amy. It's not going to work out the way you had planned. "So, how did it go?" She clasps her hands together like she's won a prize and can't wait to get her hands on it.

"Amy, I love you, I do." I give her a hug, sad to burst her bubble. "But you've got to stop trying to get me a boyfriend."

She pulls back, glancing between Ronnie and me. "Wait, what are saying?"

Over her shoulder, I see Silas quietly observing. It's a good thing she can't see her brother, because I'm sure she would be able to detect his jealousy. It's Ronnie that saves me from having to answer my best friend. "I think what she's trying to say is that she's not ready to date." He nods toward the front door. "It's getting late, we should head out."

Amy pouts. "But Ronnie is one of the good ones."

"I know." I give her another hug. On this I agree, he is a good one. "But I'm not the right one for him."

It doesn't escape my notice that Silas physically relaxes when I speak those words. Like he needed to hear them in order to breathe easy. Doesn't he know by now that I want no one other than him? He's it for me. Now that his fears have been put to rest, he turns his back to us, closing the curtain while I say goodbye to his sister.

The two of us stand on the porch, waving as Amy and Ronnie get into her car and back out of the drive. We stand outside until her taillights fade into the distance. It's quiet out, the only noises are the sounds of nature and cars off in the distance.

"So, you let him down, huh?" Silas smirks and I can't help but roll my eyes.

"Yes, butthead, I let him down." Turning to leave, I'm caught off guard when Silas grabs my wrist and tugs me to him.

"Good." That's all he says, just the one word. Then he crashes his lips down on mine, kissing me on the porch, under the stars. It's gentle and possessive all at once, and it's everything I crave.

EIGHTEEN
Silas

It has been a couple weeks since the incident with my sister and her friend, Ronnie. She has not stopped trying to set Monika up on a blind date though. Thankfully, Monika has refused my sister's lame attempts at matchmaking. Otherwise, I'm sure I would be a ticking time bomb right now. My jealousy at seeing her with Ronnie out on my porch damn near gave me a stroke.

Luca has become the king of my clinic. He has his own cozy cat tower in the corner of the back room where he lounges ninety percent of the time. The staff all love him, and spoil him rotten. He looks forward to his frequent treats and new toys.

Now that his paw is all healed up, Monika has been leash training him. At first, I didn't think it was possible. Cats hate harnesses and leashes, but Luca is happy to wear the tiny harness. Honestly, I think he is so grateful that Monika saved him, he is willing to do whatever makes her happy.

We still get suspicious stares when we arrive at work together. I'm pretty sure everyone here knows our secret. How can they not when I call Monika to my office several times a day, closing the blinds and locking the door, just so I can steal a kiss here and there.

Luckily, Amy has been super busy at the diner now that three of the waitresses quit. Not that I want my baby sister working like a dog to keep up with customer flow. But it has kept her from coming to my house unannounced and letting herself in at all hours. Though, her busy schedule doesn't prevent her from texting Monika daily with pictures of guys and invitations for blind dates.

At some point, we will have to tell my sister about us. We cannot keep going behind her back. Monika is sure that telling Amy will sabotage everything. Their friendship, and our sibling relationship. There is always the possibility that my sister will fly off the handle. Then again, it's possible she will see this as the blessing it is.

Either way, I'm not letting Monika go. She has taken up residence in my heart. The only way I would walk away from her is if she decided I wasn't who she wanted. That is a real possibility and just thinking about it pierces my heart. We have never discussed labels or what we want for the future, but damnit, I want to keep her.

Today we had two cats and four dogs that were admitted for spay and neuter, along with all of our regular patients. For sure, tonight is going to be a takeout kind of night. I doubt Monika will want to cook, and I sure as hell don't.

Five o'clock arrives swiftly, at least it feels as if it does, since we've been slammed all day. Monika discharges the last animal, a cat, and I step into the office to get charts updated and go over tomorrow's schedule. One-by-one, I hear the staff leaving for the day.

As per our routine, Monika takes out the trash and does the final walk-through to ensure the clinic is clean and ready for the next day, while I catch up on paperwork. The sound of my ringtone forces my attention off the screen. When I see Amy's name flash across the cell phone, I groan. I'm sure this call is about getting Monika back in the dating scene, again. It seems to be all she wants to talk about.

Blah, blah, blah.

I debate sending her to voicemail, but she would just call right back since she knows business hours are over. Sitting back in my chair, I swipe to answer the call. "Hello, sis."

In the background, I hear dishes clanking so I know she's at the diner. "Hey, I'm on a fifteen-minute break so I don't have long." She must be on the night shift. "Monika's birthday is coming up and I want to throw her a surprise party. Can I borrow your house? You have the biggest yard."

"Of course, you don't need my permission for that." Anything for Monika. That girl is quickly becoming my world. I never thought I would say those words, but here they are.

"Perfect." Amy answers one of her co-workers then puts the phone back to her ear. "Next Saturday. Gotta go, love you."

"Love you too." Luca prances into the office as I'm ending the call. His fluffy tail is curled back similar to how skunks arch theirs. A couple lighthearted grunts greet me before his squeaky meow. Which sounds like mer-ow-er. "Hey, little guy, where's your momma?"

Picking him up, I carry him toward the back room. Monika isn't in here, but the back door is unlocked so I set Luca on his tower and open the back door. When I do, the hairs on the back of my neck stand on end.

Monika is standing next to the dumpster, staring at the parking lot where a set of headlights shine directly on her. Since the others left nearly two hours ago, I know it's not any of my employees.

With each step toward her, the unease ramps up. This isn't right. The car doesn't move, and the headlights stay trained on Monika. A black trash bag is in her right hand, and her shoulders shake in what I can guess is fear.

When I place my hand on her shoulder, she lets out a scream that could pierce ear drums. "Shh, it's me. You're okay."

"Silas?" She turns and buries her face in the crook of my neck. Tires squeal as the car peels out of the parking lot, hopping a curb and speeding away. The bag of garbage falls to the ground and her arms wrap around my waist, squeezing for dear life.

"Come on." I wrap my arm around her waist and urge her toward the back door.

Once she is safely inside, I go back to the dumpster and toss the bag inside. Glancing back at the parking lot, there is no sign of the car that was there a moment ago. If I had a bad feeling before, its much worse now that they peeled out the way they did.

Since it's seven o'clock, it's not terribly dark out. Meaning, I was able to see the make and model of the car. Mazda CX50. I personally don't know anyone who drives one of those, but my gut tells me that Monika does.

I bet if I go in there right now and ask, she'll tell me the one name I don't ever want to hear again. Brandon. Damnit, I need to call my cousin. Why I have not done so already, I have no idea. I guess I just put it on the backburner when Monika moved in to care for Luca.

Locking the door behind me, I go in search of Monika. She's not hard to find. One peek into my office and I see her curled up in the office chair with Luca in her arms. "Hey, sweetheart, how are you holding up?"

It's a dumb question and I regret asking it the moment it leaves my mouth. With a sad smile, Monika stands from the chair. "I'll survive." Well, of that I have no doubt. This woman is one tough cookie. She's survived many trials, and I will make sure she survives any others that may arise.

"Yes, you will." Careful not to squish the kitten, I pull her into my arms and kiss the top of her head. "Care to tell me who that was?"

She shakes her head against my chest, but she answers anyway. "That was Brandon's car." Just as I had suspected. That man is about to play stupid games and win some stupid prizes. Like a reservation at the local hotel also known as county jail.

"Has this happened before?" I'm not sure how I'll feel if she says yes. I already want to murder the man with my bare hands.

"Stalk me?" she whispers.

"Yes, has he stalked you before?"

She nods and I see red. "Yes, but never quite like that." When Luca gets restless, she puts him down. "When we dated, he always had to continuously drive by to confirm my whereabouts. After we broke up, he would drive by the house or drive by the clinic, but he's never just sat there blinding me with his headlights before. Tonight was super creepy."

I agree, tonight was creepy as hell.

Unfortunately, I think tonight was just the beginning of Brandon's creepy behavior. I have a feeling he isn't done chasing after my girl.

NINETEEN
Monika

Today has been an odd day to say the least. Silas made me breakfast, that was the only normal part of my day. Then he sent me to Tulsa, an hour drive from where we live, to a day spa. I'm a simple girl, I have never been to a spa a day in my life. What does one do at these spas? Is it like the movies where everyone drinks wine while being pampered?

Tulsa isn't a city I drive to often, so I have to use GPS to navigate to the facility. My eyes spring open wide when I arrive. It's huge. Like a luxury spa you would expect to see the wealthiest people frequent. Definitely not a place I could afford to come to very often. Just staring at the building has me feeling underdressed for this occasion. Which is ludicrous, right?

Whether I'm underdressed or not, I can't drive away without getting the treatment Silas graciously prepaid for. That would be rude and a waste of money. I'm curious what my treatment will be. For all I know, he could have sent me here for a twenty-minute massage. Not going to lie, even if it is just a twenty-minute massage, I am going to get that much needed treatment. Stress is tough on the body.

Mustering up the courage, I gather my purse and walk inside. A woman in dark blue scrubs greets me as I approach the front desk. She's young and beautiful, with a body I can only hope to have some day. Her red hair is up in a messy bun that works to enhance her beauty. "Hi, how can I help you?"

"Hi." I glance around at the wide-open space with big cozy chairs. "I have an appointment."

"Perfect." A sweet smile graces her face. "What's the name?"

Surely Silas put the appointment under my name. Right? It would be stupid to book an appointment for me under his name. Wouldn't it? "Monika Grayson."

"Grayson, Grayson, Grayson." She scrolls through the names on her computer, chanting my last name.

Feeling way out of my element here, I give her the only other name it would be under. "Maybe it's under Silas McKade."

"McKade. Yep, there you are, and I see a note that this appointment is for Monika Grayson." Whew, there for a minute I thought GPS took me to the wrong location. She taps a few keys on the keyboard and then points to one of the white, cozy chairs off to the side. "You can have a seat and your therapist will be out to get you shortly."

"Thank you." I mosey over to the chair in the corner. Nerves consume me and my foot starts tapping on the pristine white tile. Silas wanted to spoil me for my birthday, I get it, but this is over the top. Cake and ice cream would have been perfect.

"Ms. Grayson?" I look up and see a petite brunette standing in the doorway, a bright smile on her face.

I want to throw up. This is not an experience I really want to have on my own. I'm one of those people that like to do things in pairs or groups. Never alone. Returning the smile, I stand and follow her to a room with a black clinical table. Folded neatly on the table is a white robe.

"My name is Patty and I'll be taking care of you today." She motions to the robe. "Go ahead and slip out of your clothing. You can leave the panties on if you prefer. I'll be back shortly."

I'm not sure what to expect, but I undress and slip into the robe. Patty gives me just enough time to get my clothes folded on the chair before coming back. She has me untie the robe and lie face down on the table. When I'm situated, she helps me out of the sleeves and folds the top down, exposing my back.

The smell of essential oils permeates the air, relaxing me. Warm oil drizzles on my upper back and I bite my lip to hold back a moan when Patty digs deep into my tight muscles. Until now, I had no idea they were this tense.

Why have I never done this before? Stress is melting away with each stroke of her hands. After working out all the knots, she moves on to my legs and feet. I knew my feet were tender, but man, when she pushes her thumbs into the arches of my feet, it's a pain that hurts so good.

I'm half asleep when the massage is over. Patty gentle shakes me awake and guides me to another room. "This is Viola, she will be your makeup artist." Makeup artist? Just what kind of package did Silas sign me up for? I thought I was coming here for a massage and maybe some fresh nail polish.

Viola is a sweet older woman. She chats about her grandchildren while applying makeup to my face. I'll be honest, I don't wear much makeup. It's pointless to wear it at work because it's such a fast-paced environment, I would end up sweating it off. So, this is actually nice.

By the time she's done, I have smokey eyes and thick full lashes. I'm not sure what kind of mascara she used, but I'll have to get myself a tube. This stuff makes my lashes look fuller than they've looked in ten years.

After applying a dark shade of red to my lips, she caps the tube and places it in the palm of my hand. "Take this with you, you may want to refreshen the lips later."

"Thank you."

Viola walks me to the next room, which happens to be the salon room. "This is Breezie, she'll get you all styled up and ready to celebrate your big day."

Breezie is a young woman with a small baby bump. She holds out her hand. "Breezie, nice to meet you."

"Nice to meet you, I'm Monika." I sit in the tall chair and Breezie pumps the chair until I'm the right height for her.

"Do you have a specific style in mind?" She studies my hair like she knows exactly what she wants to do with it.

"Not really." I shrug. "I didn't know I was getting the full treatment today."

This puts a giddy smile on Breezie's face, and she looks at me in the mirror. "So, do I get full reign on the style?"

"Have at it. The most my hair gets styled is when I pull it back and curl the ends." It's true, I suck at fixing my hair. I don't have the patience to style it. Not to mention, styling hair is not my forte.

Breezie gets out the curling iron and several clips. I have no clue what she's planning, but I'm trusting her to make me look better than my normal clinical self. She turns me away from the mirror so I can't see what she's doing.

Because the silence is getting to me, I ask, "Do you know what you're having?"

"A boy." You can hear the pride in her voice.

The remainder of our time together is spent discussing animals and books. Two of my favorite things. I'm also pleased to find out we share the same love for MC romance and have read most of the same series.

When she turns my chair around and I see my reflection in the mirror, my mouth drops open in shock. Who knew I could look so beautiful? She gave my hair curls and pinned up the sides. After friending each other on social media, she takes me back to Patty.

The last of my visit consists of a manicure and a pedicure. Neither of which I have ever had. I choose not to do the fake nails and instead opt for painting my natural nails. In my line of work, the longer nails would just get in my way.

Walking out of the building, I feel like a whole new person. Hell, I look like a whole new person. Best birthday gift ever. I'm walking on cloud nine, nothing can get me down. That is, until I pull the note from behind my windshield wiper.

Quit playing house. Your ass is mine and I'm coming for you.

Every ounce of happiness I felt just seconds ago vanishes

instantly. Who would do such a thing? Brandon? Maybe, but the note doesn't mention anything about my weight, so I'm not so sure. But, who else could it be?

With shaky hands, I unlock my car and get in. If this person is still hanging around, I don't want to give him the opportunity to get to me. Starting the car, I pull out of my parking space and leave. Every few seconds, I glance in the rear-view mirror to see if any cars are following me. It doesn't appear so, but how the hell would I know. They could be following from way back and I would never know.

Needing to talk to Silas, I grab my cell phone and search for his name while keeping my eyes on the road. The last thing I need is to wreck and leave myself wide open for this psycho to snatch me or kill me.

When his name pops up, I hit the call button. It rings and rings. "Come on, Silas, pick up the phone." The clinic is closed today, so I know he's not busy with work. After the fourth ring, I end the call and redial. "Pick up, pick up, pick up."

Panic is starting to creep in. My entire body is shaking, making it difficult to steer my vehicle. Fear's icy fingers grip me like a vice, sending shivers down my spine. Tears blur my vision but I'm too afraid to pull over. Afraid of the unthinkable.

Blinking the tears away, I pull up Amy's number. It rings twice then goes to voicemail. Surely, she didn't just send me to voicemail rather than answer. That's not us. Not how we treat each other. If she were working and was busy, she would have let it ring out, but she has never ended the call like that.

I try again and get the same result.

Now I'm full-on crying and I have no one to talk to. No one to help me calm down. Oh God, I think I'm going to be sick. I can feel the burn of bile rising in my throat. There is nowhere to pull over as I enter the on ramp for I44.

Spotting the coffee mug in the cupholder, I snatch it up just in time to spit out the yellow fluid as it rises up my esophagus. So disgusting. I manage to merge onto the highway without incident.

Now that my stomach is empty, my nerves settle, but just by a fraction. I'm still paranoid that I'm being followed. Though I can't prove it.

The further I drive, the more my nerves settle. There doesn't appear to be a car tailing me, and the tears begin to slow. Though, now all the makeup Viola did is a smeared mess. I look awful with mascara streaks on both cheeks. Not to mention, my eyes are puffy and bloodshot, and my face is blotchy. So not the look I was going for. Especially today of all days.

The exit for highway 75 is coming up so I turn on my blinker and merge over. The exit has a sharp curve to it, so I take it nice and slow. I'm looking over my shoulder to gage the traffic so I can merge onto the highway when my car jerks sideways.

Glancing in the rear-view mirror, I see a silver SUV rammed into the back of my car, pushing me forward. I try to gain control of the wheel, but the SUV backs off only to ram into me again. Cars honk and tires squeal.

Everything happens in slow motion.

The SUV hits me a third time, sending my vehicle sliding right onto the highway in the middle of traffic. Although several cars hit their brakes, it's too late. A loud crash and the sound of metal crunching meets my ears. My car rolls and my head slams into the driver's side window. Warm wetness drips down the side of my face and I can only imagine its blood. What else could it be?

My lungs are on fire, and I can't move my legs. I think the car door is pinning them down. Voices shout but they are drowned out by the beating of my heart. This isn't the way this day is supposed to go. Is this how my life ends? Dying in a car crash on my birthday?

Dizziness overwhelms me and my heart is beating out of control. Darkness dots the edges of my vision, and my thoughts go to Silas. I wish I could talk to him right now. If I could find my phone, I would call him again. Maybe he would answer this time and I could hear his voice one last time. I need to hear his voice.

His face infiltrates my mind just as the darkness takes over.

TWENTY
Silas

Amy showed up shortly after Monika left for the spa. She has been hard at work decorating my house for the surprise birthday party. For the most part, I have stayed out of her way. Every time I tried to help, she would lecture me on the art of decorating. So, I finally said screw it and left the work up to my sister.

Right now, I'm standing on my porch talking with my cousin. Wesley is my cousin on my dad's side, but he claims Amy as family even though they aren't blood related. I tell him about the abuse I saw Brandon unleash on Monika that night at the bar, and I tell him about the stalking incident I witnessed the other night at the clinic.

"Damn." He sips his sweet tea. "I hate to hear that. Unfortunately, I see this kind of thing all the time. Unless she comes down to the station and files a report, there's nothing I can do."

This is exactly what I don't want to hear, even though it's what I expected. What I want, is to get justice for Monika. Brandon needs to be behind bars. "Is there anything I can do until then?"

Wesley shakes his head. "No, it's all up to Monika." I feel defeated. There has to be something I can do until she files a report. "Well, you can install some security cameras around here and at the clinic. It's not much, but you'll know when he comes around." The man makes a valid point. In fact, I can get the ball rolling on that today.

Our visit is cut short when his radio goes off. He responds to the dispatcher and then he's off to take care of business. "Gotta go. See ya later."

When I enter the house, I'm met with a red-faced Amy. My sister cannot be mad at me for bailing on the decorations, she basically told me I was hindering the process. So, why the angry face? "What?" I say as I walk past her to put the now empty glass in the sink.

"Explain this to me." Amy reveals a picture frame that she was holding behind her back. She thrust it into my hands with enough force I'm afraid the glass will break in my palm.

I can feel the color leave my face when I glance down at the picture behind the glass. It's one of Monika and me. She is sitting on my lap and we're kissing. Monika took the selfie, and had it printed so she could place it on her nightstand. In my bedroom. "What were you doing in my room?" I ask.

"That's all you have to say?" Placing her hands on my chest, she shoves me, forcing me a step back. "How long have the two of you been sneaking around behind my back?"

"Look, it's not like that." The sound of my cell phone ringing cuts through our argument. Since it's in the other room, and I have a very angry Amy standing in front of me, I ignore it. If it's important they'll leave a voicemail or call back.

"Oh, it's not like that, huh?" She steps forward until we're toe-to-toe. "So, the two of you aren't sleeping together then?" My cell phone rings again, immediately after the first call. I'm tempted to step around my sister and see who is calling me, but she would just stomp after me, throwing a tantrum.

"Amy, calm down."

"Do not tell me to calm down." Jamming a finger into my chest, she snarls. "You just had to seduce my best friend and steal her away from me."

Okay, now this is getting juvenile. We are not school age children anymore. We're grown adults and Amy needs to start acting like one. "I am not stealing Monika away from you. There is no reason you two can't remain friends."

Amy's cell phone rings. One look at the caller ID and she swipes to send the caller to voicemail. "Bullshit. As my brother, she is off limits to you. Not to mention, Monika broke girl code. That is a serious offense." She tucks the phone into her back pocket.

"Yes, she broke girl code." I toss my hands up in the air. "But it's not like she's sleeping with your ex or anything."

"No, just my brother." Anger flares her nostrils. "You're going to break this off and send her back home. No more living together to co-parent a cat." A huff pushes past her lips. "I always thought that was stupid anyway." She points at where Luca is lounged on the living room carpet. "He's just a cat."

My sister's cell phone rings again. "Don't you want to get that?"

"No." Pulling the phone from her back pocket, she ends the call. Again. "That can wait for another time."

Great, I get to have my sister's undivided attention. On a normal day that's what I'd prefer, but today, when she's all pissy, I'd rather end this conversation and go about our merry ways. "Listen, we both felt horrible keeping this from you, but we needed time to figure out how to break it to you." I place my hand on Amy's shoulder. At my touch, she shrugs back out of my reach. Which hurts.

"You know what?" She turns and walks to the coat rack by the front door. Slinging her purse over her shoulder, she opens the door. "I'm out of here. The decorations are mostly done, and the cake is in the fridge. Y'all have fun."

What? Amy isn't staying for her best friend's birthday party. A party she spent all this time planning. "Are you serious right now?"

"As a heart attack." The door slams behind her as she leaves. I have never wanted to slap someone as much as I do my sister right now. Monika is her best friend. She could have put her differences aside for one night to celebrate with the one who has been by her side for most of their lives.

"Damnit," I scream. This day was supposed to be perfect. It has turned into a total shitshow, and I can't help but feel like this is all my fault. Afterall, I am the one that instigated this thing between Monika and me.

Do I regret it. Hell no. I have fallen for the one girl that I should have never laid eyes on. Now that I've had her, I never want to let her go. The relationship with my sister be damned. Of course, I don't want to lose my sister, but if she makes me choose, it will be Monika.

As for their friendship, I know that Monika will have to make the final decision. If her friendship with my sister is more important, I will honor her decision to break things off. As much as I don't want to, I will honor it.

Let's hope it doesn't come to that. I'm not sure I could continue to run the clinic with her there if she decides we can no longer be. Even though I just moved back, I would have to sell the clinic and my house to move back to the city.

Everyone from the clinic, as well as all of Monika's friends, are coming over tonight to celebrate her birthday. Walking through the house, I take note of the little things that need to be done. The banner needs to be hung and there are a few strings of lights that need to be put up on the patio.

Taking the photo back to my room and placing it on Monika's bedside table, I return to finish the last of the decorating. Just as the last of the lights go up, my cell phone rings. That reminds me of the missed calls I had earlier. Entering the house, I get my phone from the coffee table in the living room and swipe to answer the call. "Hello?"

"Is this Silas McKade?" A feminine voice comes through the line.

"Yes, it is." Who is calling me? I don't recognize the voice, or the number.

"My name is Teresa, I'm a nurse here at Mercy Memorial

Hospital." Goosebumps prick my skin. There is only one reason a nurse from a large hospital would be calling me. One of my family has been admitted. The question is who. My sister left here about an hour ago, and my parents are currently in Texas. "I have a Monika Grayson here. You were on her *in case of emergency* contacts." All blood drains from my face and I'm afraid I'll pass out from fear of the unknown.

"What happened to Monika, is she okay?" I'm already rushing to the front door.

"She was in an accident and has suffered severe injuries."

Before she can say another word, I say, "I'm on my way. Do whatever's necessary to save her life."

There is no time to waste, so instead of stopping by my sister's house to pick her up, I give her a call. Of course, she sends me straight to voicemail. *Brat.* I don't bother leaving a message, because if she is sending me to voicemail, chances are she won't listen to it until she is ready to hear my voice.

Opening the text messages, I use voice-to-text to send her a message.

> Silas: Get to Mercy Memorial. It's Monika.

Tossing the phone onto the passenger seat, I get onto the highway and drive well over the speed limit to get to the woman I love. Yes, the woman I love. Once I make it to her side, I will tell her just how I feel and make sure the whole world knows what she means to me.

Driving the hour to get there is pure agony. All the what ifs circle around in my head. The worst-case scenarios causing a knot to form in the pit of my stomach. What will I do if she doesn't make it? How will I get through the days at the clinic without her there?

Booking that spa day was meant to pamper her for the day. This was never supposed to be the outcome. Her birthday should be a celebration, not a tragedy. Why the hell didn't I go with her?

If I were there, maybe this wouldn't have happened. She wouldn't have been alone during the worst moment of her life.

The sound of my cell phone ringing cuts through my thoughts. A peek at the screen on my car shows that it's my sister. Using the hands-free option, I answer the call. Her voice spills through the car's speakers. "Silas, is Monika okay?"

"No." Turning on my blinker, I switch lanes to pass a car driving slow as molasses. "She was in an accident and is severely injured." She sucks in air and then sobs. Yeah, I know the feeling. "I'm about fifteen minutes from the hospital. Get there as soon as you can."

Sounds of my sister blowing her nose filters through the speakers and I cringe. "I'm on my way. Tell her I'm coming."

It's funny how a tragic event like this can diffuse all the anger one is holding against you. Because at the end of the day, those two are friends. Their love for on another trumps any disagreements they may have. A friendship like theirs is the glue that binds them together.

Rushing into the building, I ask for directions. The woman working the counter is kind enough to overlook my mannerisms and my disheveled state. Once I give her Monika's name, she instructs me to the second floor.

I'm frantic to get to her. Guilt of sending her on her own today is eating away at me. In a sense, I know this accident wasn't my fault, but I can't help but feel responsible all the same. The elevator takes forever to reach the second floor and my foot taps rapidly on the steel beneath it.

Not patient enough to wait for the doors to fully open, I wait until they part just enough to squeeze my body through. There are four nurses gathered around the nurses' station. Each of them typing away on their computers. When I approach, one of them stops what she's doing. "How can I help you?"

"I'm here to see Monika Grayson." Was that a tremble in my voice? I don't think I've ever been this shaken up before.

"You must be Silas." She stands and motions for me to follow her. As we walk, she talks. "I'm Teresa, I'm the one who called you earlier." We stop at the doorway to the waiting room. "Monika is up in surgery as we speak. She suffered a severe head injury, her left arm is broken, and there was some internal bleeding."

Internal bleeding and head injuries are serious. I place my hand on the wall next to me for support. "How long has she been in surgery, and do you have any updates?"

A sad smile crosses the nurse's face. It's brief, as if she knows she just gave away the severity of the situation and is trying to backtrack. "Monika went up to surgery minutes after I spoke with you. She coded twice, once on the way up to the OR, and once during surgery."

It feels like the ground is slipping out from under me. Squatting, I take a few deep breaths to calm my heart. Nurse Teresa is still standing there, looking upon me with sympathy. Handing me a small pack of tissues from her uniform pocket, she instructs me to have a seat in the waiting room.

Silence is a killer. It is slowly driving me insane. When my doorbell app notification goes off, it's a reminder that I forgot to call and cancel the party. As I pull up the feed, it confirms that it slipped Amy's mind as well.

Jose is standing on the porch, gift in hand. Turning on the microphone, I speak. "Hey, Jose." His gaze immediately drifts to the doorbell, but I don't give him time to speak. "We are cancelling the party. Monika is in the hospital. I will call you with an update as soon as I have one. If you don't mind, would you contact everyone about the change in plans?"

"Of course." As soon as those words leave his mouth, I swipe out of the app and turn my ringer off. I don't want to listen to it go off when others text or call for information. They'll know as soon as I get the update and decide to inform them.

A couple of people filter in, taking a seat on the other side of the room. No one speaks, each of us in our own worlds filled with worry and anxiety. I'm blankly staring at the wall in front me. My mind is full of worst-case scenarios. Especially after hearing that Monika has coded twice now.

I'm so lost in my thoughts that I don't notice my sister walking into the room. Not until she sits next to me and wraps her arm around mine, resting her head on my shoulder. "Has there been any updates?"

Shaking my head, I say, "No, but she's coded twice already. She has a head injury, a broken arm, and internal bleeding."

"Oh my god." Amy sniffs with an onset of tears. "Will she make it?"

"I hope so." Blowing out a breath, I rest my head in my hands. "Because I don't want to live in a world without her."

Minutes turn to hours and it feels like we've been here for years. The other people have left, leaving Amy and me the only ones in the waiting room. I'm getting up to get another cup of coffee when the doctor walks in. "Family of Monika Grayson."

Quickly tossing the Styrofoam cup in the trash, I meet the doctor at the door. "Tell me you have some good news." I need her to be okay.

"She's stable." Those two words are what my soul needed to hear. I reach out and hold my sister's hand as we listen to what the doctor has to say. "As you know, Monika suffered some severe injuries. We were able to locate the source of the bleeding. She's in ICU where we are keeping a close eye on her head injury."

Dropping my hand, Amy wrings her hands nervously. "Can we see her?"

He studies the two of us for a moment then nods. "Follow me."

TWENTY-ONE
Monika

Sandpaper. That's what my eyes feel like when I blink them open. They are so dry it borders on painful, like they're stuck to the lids and a piece of my eyeball peels away with the movement. Then there's the issue of the bright light in the room. It pierces my already tired and scratchy eyes, like a nail driving through to my skull. Between the two sensations, I'm growing nauseous.

When I blink again, movement to my right draws me out of my stupor. If it weren't for the pain, I would keep my eyes open, but I just can't. I'm not sure where I am, or why my body feels as though I went out partying and drank myself into a coma. That must have been some birthday party.

When a hand engulfs mine, I don't need to see him to know who it is. I know his touch like the back of my hand. A small smile tilts my lips. "Silas?" The need to look at him is strong, but the pain in my eyes and head accompanied by the nausea stops me from looking up at him.

"Yeah, sweetheart, I'm right here." His thumb rubs circles on the back of my hand, soothing away the ick that's residing in my stomach. Most people don't understand the importance of touch. Touch is a balm for the hurting. An umbrella of protection. Strength to the weak.

Silas's touch is all of the above.

With his hand in mine, I know I can face any challenge. Climb any mountain. Conquer any battle.

Then I hear the one voice that causes me to jerk my hand from his hold and pry my dry and scratchy eyes open. "Thank God, you're awake." Amy is standing next to Silas, dark circles under her eyes and a Styrofoam cup in hand. She nudges Silas out of the way, handing him her cup, so she can wrap her arms around me. "I was so scared."

"Sc-scared?" Damn, my throat is dryer than sand on a hot summer day. Feels like ash is residing in there. I need water in a bad way.

As if reading my mind, Silas holds a cup to my mouth, bringing the straw to my lips. "Here, take a sip." I do. At first, the cool liquid burns going down. Then the burn turns to relief as I swallow more and more of the water. Jeez, how wasted did I get last night? Normally, I don't drink like that. Bordering drunk, yes. Wasted, no.

After I drain the contents of the cup, I finally take in my surroundings. The large marker board on the wall with my name, nurse's name, and date. Then the bed with side rails. "Wait, why am I in the hospital?" At that moment, my eyes zero in on the date. "Tell me that it's not Tuesday. Somebody tell me that I didn't lose three days."

Three days. How is that possible?

Using my hands, I try to push myself up, but the excruciating pain in my abdomen stops me short. Not to mention, there's a cast on my left arm. Gasping breaths fill the room and tears spring to my eyes, somewhat soothing the dryness. What's wrong? What happened to me?

Silas is gently shoving his sister aside to be the one to help me lie back. "Easy, sweetheart. You don't want to do too much too soon."

Taking a few deep breaths to gather my bearings, I gaze up at Silas. "What do you mean, too much too soon?" At the worst possible moment, a jackhammer slams into my skull. A headache unlike any I have ever had before. I gasp and grip my head, squeezing my eyes shut.

"Shit." Silas reaches across me, jarring my body and worsening the headache. "Sorry," he says as he pushes a button on the bedrail.

A voice comes from a speaker next to my head. "How can I help you?" I want to slap whoever it is that dares to speak, adding to the pain crushing my cranium. If I wanted to puke before, it's ten times worse now.

Silas strokes my cheek as he speaks. "We need a nurse, now. Monika is awake and judging by the way she's cradling her head I'd say she's in need of pain meds."

"I'm on my way." The nurse sounds concerned, or it could have been my imagination. If my headache is anything to go by, probably not my imagination.

The pain crushing my skull gets to be too much to bear, causing the nausea to rise a notch. When the darkness comes to drag me down into the depths of its abyss, I welcome it.

This time when my eyes open, there's no stabbing pain. In fact, my whole body is nice and relaxed. So much better than last time. Last time I thought I was going to die. My whole body hurt.

Then I remember where I am.

In the hospital.

I still have no idea why I'm here. No idea if I got sick, or possibly injured somehow. Staring back at me is Silas, his gray eyes flooding with relief. He lifts my hand to his mouth, kissing my knuckles. "How's your head, sweetheart?"

"It's, uh, it's better." I try to sit up, but he quickly places a hand on my shoulder to keep me rooted to the bed. It puzzles me why he would insist I stay laying down. But the look in his pleading eyes has me obeying his silent command.

Then I notice the nurse standing on the other side of my bed.

She glances from the screen to me when I settle back against the pillow. "How are you feeling?"

"Okay." Well, that is totally a lie. My body may feel relaxed, but it's still sore and raw. "Not a hundred percent true." Glancing at Silas, I bite my lower lip because I don't want him to worry. Yet, I can't keep this from my nurse. Can I? No, it wouldn't be in my best interest. "I kind of feel like I've been through a meat grinder."

She smiles sympathetically. Though, I'm not sure why. It's not like I've been in a terrible car accident. "That is to be expected considering the injuries you've sustained."

It takes a few seconds for her words to register, but when they do, I can feel all the color leave my face. "What do you mean by injuries?" Lifting my arms, I take stock of the bruising I haven't noticed up until now. The cast on my left arm. How the hell did I miss that? Then I remember seeing it before I passed out. If my arms look this bad, how does the rest of me look? "What happened to me?"

Shock widens her brown orbs. Stepping closer, she uses a pen light to examine my eyes. "You don't remember what happened to you?"

"No." I shake my head. The motion stirring up the nausea. "The last thing I remember is going to the spa." It's then that I pause because I don't remember leaving the spa. I had just assumed that Silas took me out for my birthday, and I drank a bit too much. Which isn't like me, I still watch my calories. Not as heavily as I did before Silas, but still enough to know that too much alcohol means too much of an uptick in unnecessary caloric intake.

It's now that Amy steps into my line of sight. I hadn't seen her sitting in the corner. She comes to stand next to her brother, gently touching my thigh. Offering me her strength, like her brother who is still holding my hand. Her worried eyes take me in. "You don't remember the accident?"

"Accident?" How? When? "I don't remember." Tears blur my vision as I try to remember but come up blank.

The nurse discloses my injuries, and the surgery that I underwent. "It was due to your head injury that we had you sedated for forty-eight hours."

Amy and Silas are quiet, each touching me, offering their strength and support. Silas holding my hand and Amy's hand on my leg. I don't know what I would do without the two of them. These two are my family. The only family that matters to me. Amy is my sister, maybe not by blood, but blood is not what makes a family. Then there's Silas. He's my heart, my home. Dare I say, the one I love above all else. He's the one I cannot live my life without.

Without him, I do not exist.

Just as the nurse finishes detailing my injuries, the doctor walks in. "Good to see you awake." With his own pen light, he examines my eyes and then glances at the computer screen, reading my chart. No doubt looking at my vitals to determine how my body is coping.

"Is my head okay?" I tighten my hold on Silas's hand as I direct my questions at the doctor. "Why do I not remember the accident?"

The doctor sits on the stool and wheels himself closer to the bed. "Memory loss is not uncommon for patients who have experienced the level of injuries you have." He takes my good hand and places his first two fingers on my inner wrist, counting my pulse. "You'll likely regain those memories in the next day or two. Nothing to worry about."

Easy for him to say, he's not the one suffering. Not the one who can't remember the events leading up to the accident that caused such a trauma.

After discussing treatments, the doctor leaves with the nurse trailing along behind him. Now it's just Amy and Silas here to fill the otherwise quiet room. My best friend looks like she's on the fence about whether she wants to be here. I'm sure she has a shift at the diner to get to.

Not wanting her to feel as though she has to spend every

minute with me in the hospital, I give her the go ahead to leave if she wants. "Amy, you don't have to stay here if you have something else you need to do."

Finally, she looks over at me. "What? No, I'm not going anywhere."

"You sure?" I question, because she honestly looks like she'd rather be anywhere else but here. "You don't seem all too keen on being here."

"Don't be silly." Amy glances at her brother then back to me. "I'm just worried about you, that's all."

The look that passes between Amy and Silas could be considered a silent conversation. He raises an eyebrow, and she purses her lips before lifting her own brow. Silas has since let go of my hand, but his hand has never left my shoulder, where his touch is almost possessive.

TWENTY-TWO
Silas

Monika is finally being discharged after nearly two weeks in the hospital. Since I refused to leave her side, the clinic has only been open for routine visits. All surgeries have been put on hold. The only exception being the one emergency surgery that came in two days ago. Jose was able to get in touch with Doctor Allen, who was gracious enough to fill in.

As the car comes to a stop, Monika takes in the deflated balloons around the exterior of the house. Then her eyes trail over to the spot where she normally parks her car. The spot has been sitting empty since her birthday. Since she drove away for her spa appointment.

A damn spa appointment.

I will never again send her anywhere without me by her side. When I got the call that she had been in an accident, I thought my life was over. The fear of losing her rocked my world so hard that I couldn't breathe.

In that moment I knew. I knew that I could never live in a world where she wasn't. This girl that was supposed to be off limits, the forbidden fruit, is the other half of my heart. The connecting piece to my soul.

Amy and I have not talked about my relationship with Monika since the day we argued. The day that the both of us ignored Monika's calls as she feared for her life. After finding a note attached to her windshield in a parking lot. Calls that came just minutes before her accident.

I'm not sure I will ever be able to forgive myself for not answering her that day. By not picking up the phone, I feel as though I failed her. As though the accident was all my fault. Yes, I know how irrational that sounds, there is no way I could have prevented the accident just by picking up the phone. That wreck would have happened even if I were on the phone with her. Yet I can't help but feel guilty.

She stares at the spot that used to be hers. The spot that is now void of her vehicle. Sadness sweeps across her face, and I want to wipe it away. Want to bring joy back into her life. "Hey." Pinching her chin, I turn her face toward me. Her watery eyes are damn near my undoing. "Don't worry about that right now."

Tears fill her eyes and my heart aches for what she's gone through. No one should have to go through what she has. It's not fair. Especially for someone as pure as Monika. Anger boils under the surface, rage flowing through my veins at the hand she's been dealt. I would straight up walk on burning coals embedded with shards of sharp glass, barefoot, for this girl.

Rest assured, I will burn the world down to make sure she gets the justice she deserves. This woman deserves so much more than the shit she's been handed. If it takes everything I've got, I will make sure the rest of her life is filled with nothing but the best life has to offer.

She means more to me than my clinic. Hell, she means more to me than my own life. And yes, I realize claiming her could very well cost me where my sister is concerned. As they say, the heart wants what the heart wants. Monika is the other half of my heart and if Amy can't accept that, then that's all on her.

Leaning forward, I give her a chaste kiss then exit the vehicle to help her out. She's slow pushing herself out of the car, even with me helping her. I can tell by the sweat dotting her forehead, and the grimacing, that she's in need of a pain pill. She hates taking them because she doesn't want to become addicted like her mother did after her father's death. I get that, I do. But if I see her unable to relax due to pain, I will make sure she takes one to ease the discomfort.

It takes her a couple of minutes to get to the porch. Taking one look at the stairs, she groans. "I'm not sure I have the energy. Go ahead, I'm just going to stand here for a minute."

If she thinks I'm going to let her stand out here alone and in pain, she's wrong. Even if I were dying of thirst, I would not leave her for a second. Pressing my lips into a thin line, I jog up the steps and unlock the front door, pocketing my keys as I descend. Bending, I lift her bridal style.

Surprise widens her eyes. "What are you doing?"

"Carrying you." As I cross the threshold, I kick the door shut behind me.

Her eyes search mine. "I can see that, but why?"

A fresh wave of anger swims in my veins. Why has no one cared for this woman properly? It should not be an anomaly to be cared for. Yet, she acts as though she isn't worth it. I will make it my life's mission to show her how she should be taken care of. "Because I refuse to leave my woman outside alone."

"Wait." Once her feet hit the floor, she reaches for my hand. "What exactly are you saying?"

Not wanting her to have doubts, I tell her the truth. "You're mine. No more hiding our relationship. You are mine, and I'm yours. Every need you have is mine to fulfil. When you hurt, I will be there to take care of you."

She worries her bottom lip. "What about Amy? We can't do that to her."

Helping her to the sofa so she can sit and relax is priority. Once she settles in, I hand her the bottle of pain medicine. When she shakes her head, I set the bottle on the end table next to her. Then I sit on the edge of the coffee table so I can hold her hands and look into her eyes. "First of all, we aren't doing anything to Amy. Second, I refuse to throw away the other half of me because my sister doesn't want me to date her best friend. I would rather cut off my own limbs."

Those blue orbs mist over, and she smiles. "So, we're doing this?"

I nod. "Yes, no more hiding. If I've learned anything from your accident, it's that I can't live without you." She opens her mouth, but I place a finger to her lips. "I want this with you, Monika. I want the world to know you're mine." Those words have been on the tip of my tongue all week, but I had wanted to wait for the right moment. This may not be the right moment, but it needs to be said. I need her to know I'm serious about us.

Slipping one hand free, she places it over her heart. "I have wanted this for so long."

"Yeah, me too." Those tears that have been pooling in her eyes finally spill over. With the pad of my thumbs, I wipe the wetness away then move to her side so I can wrap my arm around her.

Turning her face toward mine, I see the concern in her gaze. Monika closes her eyes as she whispers. "Amy is going to hate me."

No doubt my sister will give Monika a piece of her mind. I'm almost certain that she has plans to continue our argument from that weekend. From the day Monika had her car accident. I'm still sad and angry at the both of us for what we did that day. Amy and I both ignored those calls that came through right before she was hit by another car. A car that drove off and left her alone to die.

"She'll be mad," I admit. "But she will get over it. You're her best friend, y'all have been through too much to throw that away." Reaching out, I brush a stray lock of hair behind her ear. "And she can't escape me, I'm her brother."

"I hope she forgives me." Stopping short, she looks around, frowning. "Where is Luca?"

When she goes to push herself up from the sofa, I place a hand on her thigh. "Jose will bring him home in a few. He's been taking care of him for us."

Relief washes over her. "Oh, thank goodness. I bet my poor

baby would have been so lonely if he had been left here all by himself."

"Yes," I agree. "He would have been lonely, and sad."

Our moment ends when the front door swings open and Amy steps inside. Her gaze takes in our closeness and my arm around Monika. "Well, I see you two are nice and cozy."

Monika immediately moves out from under my arm. Guilt washing over her face. This is clearly not how she wanted my sister to find out about us, that much is clear by the expression on her face. What she doesn't know is that Amy already knows about us. So, what my sister is seeing is not a shock to her. "Amy." Monika's voice is a near whisper.

Amy, feigning shock, places a hand over her heart. "Care to explain what is going on here, bestie?" Even for me, her own brother, it's hard to tell whether Amy is truly upset or just acting. Surely, she's had time to cool down and think this through. I would like to think my sister wouldn't throw away years of friendship over some stupid girl code. The whole *not dating your best friend's sibling* is absurd.

Monika pales. "I, um." Poking her tongue out, she wets her lips. "Um." Letting out a puff of air, she takes a deep breath and continues. "Why don't you sit, we need to talk."

I eye my sister closely, looking for any signs that she is about to lose her shit. Her poker face is firmly in place, I can't get a read on her mood. Which is slightly unnerving. An emotionless Amy can be scary, you never know if you're getting the rational Amy or the one ready to tear the world a new one.

Amy pushes the coffee table back and takes a seat on it, directly in front of Monika, crossing her legs and leaning forward to stare at her best friend. "I'm sitting." She blows a bubble with her gum. "Now, spill it."

This is painful to watch. I hate seeing Monika tied up in knots over telling my sister about us. So, I intervene. "Amy, stop."

"Nu, uh." She side eyes me. "I want to hear what Monika has to say."

Of course, she does. My sister gets off on watching others suffer. I swear she would make a good cop or lawyer. She most definitely has the right demeanor for it. Instinct has me wanting to take over this conversation and shield Monika from my sister. Experience with Amy keeps me silent. If I intervene further then she will drill Monika harder, and with her still delicate from her injuries, there is no way I'm making this worse for her.

Monika grabs a pillow from the corner of the sofa and tucks it behind her back on the injured side. "Silas and I have been seeing each other."

Amy leans back, tapping her thigh with her thumb. "And how long has this been going on?"

"I never meant to betray you." Monika shifts, doing her best to hide a grimace, but I see it. By the looks of it, Amy does too, because her eyes soften. "Amy, I never set out to break girl code. It just sort of happened."

Amy's eyebrow rises. "So, you never lusted after my brother as a kid?"

"I—" Monika looks confused. So am I. "Wait, you knew I had a crush on your brother back then?"

Amy huffs. "Of course, why do you think I told you that you could never crush on this bum?"

"Oh." Monika lowers her gaze to her legs, pink tinting her cheeks.

"Again," Amy goes on. "How long have you two been seeing each other?"

I am two seconds away from throwing my sister out of my house. The only thing preventing me from doing so, is the fact that these two need to work this out. It's either now or later, and I know that Monika will be miserable if they don't finish this now that it's out in the open.

Monika's gaze never leaves that spot on her thighs. No doubt not wanting to see the disappointment on my sister's face when she tells her the truth. Even though Amy already knows because we've already had this argument. "Since we rescued Luca and I moved into his guest bedroom."

Amy throws her hands up in the air. "I can't believe you."

TWENTY-THREE
Monika

Amy tosses her hands in the air, slapping them on her thighs. "I can't believe you."

This is exactly why I should have never kissed Silas that night at Andromeda. I knew then that if I had one taste, I would want another and another. For the rest of my life, I would want him with a fierceness that is impossible to resist. Especially now that I've fallen in love with him. "Amy, I'm sorry I hurt you, but it is what it is."

"You broke the one rule, the only rule actually." Amy doesn't raise her voice, but you can hear the disappointment in her tone. A disappointment that causes my shoulders to slump in guilt.

I hate that I've ruined our friendship. That was never my intention. "I never meant to, Amy. I swear." Let's pray I can salvage this, so I don't lose my best friend. "It all started with a kiss to get Brandon off my back. He was harassing me, saying that no man would ever want me. Silas stepped in and kissed me to throw those words back in his face."

Amy holds up a hand to stop me. "Wait, Brandon did what now?"

Silas speaks before I can utter another word. "That bastard was spewing hateful words at her, and I was not going to stand by and listen to him tear her down."

"I never did like that asshole." Amy places her hand on my knee. "He was never good enough for you." She doesn't even know half it. I've never shared with her the lengths Brandon would go to just to tear me down and keep me in line. Never mind the times he was physical with me. That's not something I'm proud of.

"I know that now," I admit. Before Silas, I didn't understand this fact. Brandon conditioned me from the beginning of our relationship, and I just believed the hatred he drilled into me. It wasn't until Silas started breaking down those hate filled walls and speaking truth that I began to see my worth. I have him to thank for my new take on life.

"Good." Amy looks between Silas and me. "But we need to discuss this thing between the two of you. It can't go on. I mean, the age difference for one."

"It's four years," Silas says. "It's not like I'm a twenty-eight-year-old man preying on a teenager."

"That may be, but the two of you will never work." Amy's pleading eyes land on me. "You are vulnerable right now and on the rebound." Yet she has been relentlessly trying to hook me up. Those hazel pools land on her brother now. "And you are not the settling down type. You can't commit, and then where will that leave her?" She points at me while staring her brother down.

"So, that's what this is about? My lack of commitment in the past?" Silas leans forward, invading his sister's space. "I will have you know that the reason for my noncommitment is because I had not found the right woman. Not until Monika."

A snigger comes from Amy. "And what, you finally found the right woman in her?"

"Yes, I have." Silas shifts, closing his eyes for a moment before speaking again. When he does, his voice is soft. "I love her, Amy, and there is nothing you can say that will force me away from her."

Amy speaks but I don't hear her over the beating of my own heart. Did he just say what I think he did? My best friend is still going on and on, but what she is saying is meaningless. In this moment, my sole focus is on Silas. On the fact he is shining a light on our relationship.

Touching his arm, I gain his attention. "Say that again." I have to hear him say it again in order to believe what I've just heard.

He moves off the sofa, nudging his sister to scoot over. There is a little hesitation from her, but she finally moves out of the way. Once she does, Silas kneels in front of me. Brushing a lock of hair behind my ear, he takes my hands, running his thumbs over my knuckles. "I have fallen in love with you, Monika."

My heart soars because this has been my dream since I was fourteen years old. The one thing I never thought would happen. Yet here he is, confessing his love for me. I hear a gasp coming from my left but don't dare break eye contact with this man. Cupping his face, I give him my truth. "I love you too."

Smiling, he leans forward and rests his forehead against mine. "You do?"

"I do." Tilting my head, I kiss him, not caring that his sister is standing here, witnessing our affection. He deepens the kiss and as our tongues tango, it's like coming home. He is my home. My world. The one I cannot live without.

"Okay, that's enough." Amy claps her hands obnoxiously. "A sister should not be subject to such behavior." She mutters something about us being disgusting, which causes Silas and me to chuckle. When we finally pull away from each other, Amy is staring at us with her arms crossed over her chest. "So, this is really happening?"

"Yes," Silas and I say at the same time.

"You really love her?" She questions her brother.

Silas stands and squares his shoulders as he faces Amy. "With my whole heart."

Amy worries her bottom lip as she glances from me to Silas and back again. "Well, hell." She tosses her hands up in the air. "I guess I have no choice but to accept this." Then she takes a step toward her brother, jamming her pointer finger into his chest. "If you so much as think about hurting my bestie, I will kill you myself."

I laugh because that is Amy. Always protective. This is why I love her. She has stuck up for me from day one. Even against her once best friend when she dared to call me a walrus back in middle school.

"I would expect nothing less," Silas says.

With that, she sits beside me on the sofa, gently wrapping me in her arms. When I wince, she pulls back and apologizes. "Sorry."

"Don't be." I lean against her shoulder; thankful she isn't ending our friendship over this. "So, we're okay?"

"Yeah, we're okay." She rests her head on mine. "I couldn't think of a better person for my brother." There's a small pause. "It's weird and a tad bit gross because he's my brother and I don't want to think about his love life, but I'm glad it's you."

Happiness like I've never known overwhelms my senses and tears spill from my eyes. I feel like all I do is cry. As they drip onto her shoulder, wetting the fabric, she pulls away and turns her worried gaze onto my face.

Silas is also staring at me like something is wrong, or like he thinks I might be in pain. I'm not. Well, I am, but that's not the reason for my tears. "It's okay guys. I'm just happy." I wipe the tears away. "I found love and I have my best friend by my side."

They both smile.

Amy stands, "Well, I got so caught up in this whole situation that I completely forgot why I came in the first place." Curious, I wait for her to explain. When she heads over to the front door, I frown, wondering why she's leaving. Then she picks up the plastic bag that she set on the floor when she entered.

I recognize the logo on the front. It's from the diner she works at. Surprise, surprise. She's always bringing us food from work. "You brought food?"

She nods. "I also got you a salad." Of course, she did. Salad is about the only thing I've eaten since dating Brandon. "And steak, fries, and mac n' cheese for this bonehead," she waves a hand toward her brother.

Rolling his eyes, Silas takes the bag. "Thank you." Tossing his arm over my shoulder, he beams at his sister, my best friend. "Are you joining us?"

"Duh." Amy waltzes past us. "You didn't think I was going to sit here and watch the two of you eat, did you?" She busies herself with plates and silverware. When Silas splits his food with me, adding some of the salad to both of our plates, Amy turns a questioning gaze my way.

I just smile and cut a piece of steak, popping it in my mouth. Amy doesn't touch her meatball sub as she watches me eat. Halfway through the meal, I can't take it any longer. "Chill, you're being creepy."

Pointing at my plate and shaking her head, she says, "I'm sorry, but I haven't seen you eat like that in a very long time."

I hang my head in shame because of what I allowed Brandon to do to me. "I know." It took a lot for Silas to show me how my ex conditioned me. How badly he tore me down with his words. I never realized how much his actions had changed me. Not until Silas took the time to show me. He has taught me to love myself again. To enjoy the foods that I once loved but denied myself.

Silas kisses the side of my head. "We have been working on that."

Amy finally takes a small bite. "I'm glad to see some of the old you again." She doesn't say what I know she wants to. That Brandon is the loser that is to blame for the shell I became. I'm thankful she doesn't voice it. That man has ruined my life for long enough. I don't want to think about him ever again.

The next two weeks seem to drag by. Silas returned to work the Monday after I was discharged from the hospital. So, I have been spending my days at home, watching television, and cuddling with Luca. No housework since Silas has forbidden me from lifting a finger. To ensure I keep to his instructions, he has hired a cleaner to come in daily.

Boring.

I'm recovering from injuries, not on my deathbed. Jeez, the man drives me up the frickin' wall with his overprotectiveness. I swear, if he doesn't let up a little, I'm going to hit him over the head with a frying pan. At least I have Luca to keep me company and prevent me from going insane.

This ragdoll kitten is the best thing in my life, other than Silas. Luca is my little furry companion. We have conversations. Well, conversations of sorts. I talk and he grunts. When he's in a talkative mood, he meows. Those cute meows sound like mer-ow-er. It's the cutest thing ever.

Though he only has half his tail, it is so fluffy it kind of reminds me of a skunk's tail with the way he arches it over his back.

We're still waiting to hear back from Wesley about the investigation concerning my car accident. When I finally regained my memories, I told Wesley about the silver SUV. It was one I didn't recognize, so that put to rest the fear of it being Brandon. So far, no one has been able to find out who hit me. Whoever it was fled the scene and has yet to take their car in for repairs or report it to their insurance.

The note that had been left on my car was never recovered, so the police have no way of testing for prints. Unfortunately, I never tucked that note in my purse or glovebox, I just haphazardly tossed it on the passenger seat. Dumb, I know.

Silas's cousin has been very kind to me during this whole ordeal. Wesley has gathered a team of his highly trusted and talented men to work on my case. This team is working overtime to solve the mystery and get me justice. For that, I'm grateful.

Luca and I are currently reclined on the sofa watching a show about haunted houses. I love watching these and listening to the owner's talk about their experiences living there, but I could never step foot in one. The first supernatural encounter, and I would run screaming. The world wouldn't see me again because I would find a safe place to hide and never come out.

Just as a ghost pops up on the screen, a knock comes from the front door. I nearly jump out of my skin from the noise. Luca hisses and I pet him behind the ears. "It's okay, baby, momma didn't mean to scare you."

Instead of calming down, he hops off my lap and stands on the other side of the sofa, hissing toward the front door.

Knock. Knock.

"It's okay." I pet him on my way to the door. It's probably just Wesley coming to give me an update. Luca nips my ankle when I step forward. The behavior is odd, but I ignore his protest and unlock the front door, swinging it open.

Dread fills me when I do. The last person I thought I would see is standing on the other side, holding a gun.

TWENTY-FOUR
Silas

After work, I stop by the grocery store to pick up some broccolini, chicken, and ingredients for a salad. Even though Monika is now enjoying her favorite foods in bigger portions, she still prefers to have a nice salad before meals to prevent herself from overeating the higher calorie foods. It frustrates me to no end, but hey, at least we're moving in the right direction. A little more each week. So that's a plus.

Tonight is a special night because I have a surprise for her. A brand-new black Volvo XC40. We have an appointment to go in tomorrow morning and pick it up. I know she will put up a fight on this car because she is very independent and prefers to take care of herself. Which is a great quality to have, but on this, I will not budge. As my woman, I have the privilege of providing for her, and I intend to do just that.

Whistling, I load the shopping cart with the necessary groceries. Midway down the aisle, my cell phone rings. I slip the device from my back pocket to check the caller ID. It's Wesley. If not for the fact he is working on Monika's case, I wouldn't bother answering the call right now, but something tells me this is important.

"Hey, man. What's up?"

"Hey, you free to meet with me?" My cousin sounds exhausted. Which makes me wonder if he is getting adequate rest, or if he's working himself to the bone to solve Monika's case. As his cousin, I want him to put his health first, but as Monika's boyfriend, I want his sole focus on this case. I have very mixed emotions about it.

Eyeing the items in the shopping cart, I blow out a breath then answer his question with a question. "How urgent is this meeting? I was planning a nice dinner for Monika."

"I don't mean to intrude on your plans." He blows out a puff of air. "But I think we need to talk ASAP. I might have a lead on who hit Monika."

Damnit, I knew this was about her case. Part of me is happy he has a lead, and part of me is a nervous wreck. "Where?" With one hand, I push the cart to a store associate. "Sorry, I have to leave." The associate glares at me for dumping my load on him, but I would rather he put it away than leave it to sit and spoil.

"Your place, I'm leaving the station now." Without a goodbye, Wesley ends the call.

The urgency in his voice quickens my steps. Hopefully this is the break we need to get my woman the justice she deserves. Driving to the house feels like eternity, and my blood pressure is spiking from thoughts of the unknown.

I don't know how he beat me, but Wesley is stepping from his truck when I pull up. He looks more exhausted than he sounded over the phone. Dark circles outline his eyes, and his hair is unkempt.

"Hey." He follows me as I ascend the steps.

"Hey." Holding the door open, I motion for Wesley to enter. "Want something to drink?" I ask him as I scan the living room for Monika. Normally, she is sitting on the sofa with Luca on her lap.

"Coke, if you have one." Wesley sits on a barstool at the island.

Sliding a bottle of Coke toward him, I say, "Give me a second, I'm going to check on Monika."

"No problem."

Passing the guest room, I peek inside the open room. Empty,

like I expect it to be. The door to the hall bathroom is open and the lights are off, indicating she is not in there. Entering our bedroom, I spot Luca perched on the end of the bed. When he sees me, he immediately starts meowing. Not a normal meow, but one of distress.

"Hey there, furball." Figuring he's hungry, I pick him up so I can take him to the kitchen with me. "Monika?" I call out. Opening the master bathroom door, I notice it's empty as well.

Interesting. It's not like she can go anywhere, she doesn't have a vehicle. Not unless Amy came over to give her lift. Carrying Luca to the kitchen, I put food in his bowl. Instead of eating, he waltzes to the front door, meowing like he's crying out for help. I've never seen him behave this way.

Dialing my sister, I put the phone to my ear as I continue to watch Luca. Amy answers on the third ring. "Hey, what's up?"

"Is Monika with you?" When I ask this, Wesley turns around and raises a brow.

"No." *Clang.* The sound of pots clanging against each other tells me she is at work. "I spoke with her earlier on my break. Why, is she not answering her phone?"

"I haven't tried calling her, I just figured she was with you since she's not home." At this, Wesley pulls his cell phone out of his back pocket and dials a number. *Ring, ring, ring.* Stepping into the living room, I see Monika's phone on the coffee table next to half a glass of tea. "Shit. I gotta go."

"Wait," Amy shouts just as I'm about to end the call. "What's going on?"

Wesley stands and pockets his phone.

"Monika is missing." I unlock the device and scroll through her calls and texts to see if I can find a clue as to where she might have gone, and who she might be with. "Her phone is here, but she's nowhere to be found."

"Okay, calm down." A door closes and then the clanging of dishes disappears. "Have you looked on the back patio?"

"Not yet." Wesley follows me outside and we search the property. Moving the cell phone away from my mouth, I yell for her. "Monika?" Wesley goes left of the house, and I go right. Each of us calling her name.

Faintly, I can hear someone yelling my name and it takes me a few seconds to realize its coming from my hand. In searching for Monika, I had forgotten I was on a call with my sister. She's frantic by the time I get the device back to my ear. "Silas Conrad McKade."

"I'm here." Running back to the front of the house, Wesley is shaking his head when he rounds the corner. "Shit. She's not here."

"I'm on my way." Amy ends the call and I place my hand over my pounding heart.

This is unlike Monika to leave without letting me know. All the worst-case scenarios flash through my thoughts. Each one spiking my heartrate further. Opening the app on my cell phone, I go through the history on our surveillance system.

The camera above the garage picks up a red vehicle turning into our driveway, but then the footage turns to static before I can make out the model. This raises the hairs on my arms. Opening the saved videos from the doorbell camera reveals nothing but static. I have a feeling this is foul play.

Nausea sours my stomach as I fret over Monika's safety.

Wesley is standing beside me, viewing the footage alongside me. When I look over at him, his lips are pressed into a thin line. "We need to talk. Now."

TWENTY-FIVE
Monika

My head is pounding, and bile is sitting at the base of my esophagus, threatening to rise to the surface. Ugh, I feel like I have been through the meat grinder. Again. Every inch of my body hurts. Lifting my arm so I can press my fingers to my temple is a chore. My limbs feel as though they are made of lead.

What the hell is wrong with me?

Cracking an eye open, I see the interior of the car that I'm in. I try to lift my head but it's like my skull is a bowling ball. All I can manage is to tilt my head a fraction. When I do, I see it. A stain on the back of the driver's seat. A stain I know all too well. One that leaves a sour taste in my mouth.

That brown stain is from Brandon spilling his coffee while loading boxes in the back of his Mazda.

I remember that day like it was yesterday. It was the first time he physically hurt me. He had grabbed my hair and jerked me away from the car, screaming at me for spilling his coffee. Blaming me because I was standing next to him, therefore I must have bumped into him, ruining his brand-new car.

It had terrified me because he had never been physical with me before. Complained about my weight, yes, but he hadn't laid a finger on me until that day. I can still remember the way my heart felt like it would beat right through my chest. It beat so loudly that his screaming became background noise.

His temper rose so quickly, like a flip of a switch. I had never witnessed such a change in a person before then. When you see that kind of behavior acted out on television, you have a tendency to believe its overexaggerated. That a human could not possibly be so cruel to the ones they love.

That day I learned the hard way. One, never judge a book by its cover. Kindness on the surface doesn't mean their heart is kind. Two, just because they love you, or claim to love you, doesn't mean they won't lash out at you.

After screaming in my face, he shoved me into the side of the brick house and backhanded me. Demanding I clean up the mess I had made. I tried to get all the coffee out of the fabric, but the damage had already been done. As punishment, he went out and got all my favorites from the Chinese restaurant in the next town over and made me sit at the table and watch him eat it all. And that was the beginning of my new Brandon approved diet. Eating basic salads, and only eating enough to quiet the growling of my stomach but never more than a fist full.

Looking back on those times, I can't believe I allowed him to abuse me for so long. How had I not seen his behavior as abusive? It astonishes me how easily I accepted his apologies after every physical altercation. How I just accepted that it was my fault. That I angered him to the point he had no control.

Thank God Silas has shown me differently. He has helped me understand that I had been conditioned. Brainwashed. Because of him, I now know that I am worth more than I ever knew, and I deserve the world. Yes, there are times when I falter, but Silas is right there to remind me of my worth.

A flick of a zippo pulls me from my thoughts. When I glance up at the rearview mirror, I find brown eyes staring back at me. "Good, you're awake."

Those eyes and the sound of his voice is all it takes for it all to come crashing back.

I remember opening the front door to discover my worst nightmare smiling back at me. The flash of pure evil in his eyes as he looked me up and down. Then the punch to the side of the head. Which is most likely the root cause of the headache I currently have. Then nothing as unconsciousness took over.

Even through all of that, my first concern is for my cat. Did he close the front door? If he didn't, did Luca run out of the house and get lost. Is my little bundle of fur okay? "My cat?" Those two words come out rough. My throat is so dry, it's like I'm trying to swallow cotton.

His brown pools narrow on me. "That little shit bit me. He's lucky I didn't break his neck before throwing his ass back inside the house." My silence must anger him because his next words come out on a growl. "You should really thank me for not killing your stupid cat."

As much as I want to defy him, I know that now is not the time. Not while we are in a moving vehicle and my body is slow to move, almost like I've been drugged. Which is highly possible considering how unhinged Brandon seems to be. "Thank," *cough,* "you." *Cough.* The more I speak, the drier my throat feels.

Yep, I have definitely been drugged. The question now is, how will I escape. Knowing Brandon, he will not wait long to drug me again. He will not want to take the risk of me running. Keeping eye contact, I carefully reach for my back pocket in hopes my cell phone is there.

It isn't. Damn, there goes my hope of Silas being able to track my location.

A sharp turn causes me to roll off the back seat and I groan when my shoulder connects with the floor. Like the sick bastard he is, Brandon chuckles at my pain. How did I live with him all those years? I always thought I had more sense than that, but I guess when you've been brainwashed, you don't know any better.

"Where are we going?" I would like to think Brandon will come to his senses and let me go. Surely, he doesn't want to face a kidnapping charge. Maybe he is just unleashing his anger by scaring me and at the end of the day he will take me home.

"You'll see soon enough." He flips the lid to his zippo several times before tossing it into the center console. "Don't even think about trying to get away." He turns around briefly to look down at me. "I have enough sedatives to last for days."

Days? I don't want to be his prisoner for days. All I want is to be set free.

My head slides into the door when Brandon takes a turn. The car jostles me around as we travel along a gravel road. All the motion is upsetting my stomach and I close my eyes, breathing deeply to alleviate the queasiness.

I'm so focused on my breathing that I don't realize that the car has stopped. Not until the backdoor opens and hands grip me by the arms, pulling me from the vehicle. My body hits the ground with a thud, and I groan. My arm was just healing up, now I'm going to be sore all over again.

Brandon grips me under my shoulders and drags me. "Damn, you're heavy as hell." There was a day when those words would have hit me so hard. I would have apologized, cut back more calories, and ramped up my cardio. Not now. Now I have some confidence and self-love.

My toes flex when he drags me up the porch steps. I wonder if the drugs are starting to wear off. To test this, I wiggle my toes while his focus is on the steps behind him. Now that my thoughts have shifted and my mind is attuned to my body, I realize that my limbs no longer feel like lead. Achy, but no longer heavy.

Not wanting to give anything away, I don't move. Once we cross the threshold, I recognize where we are. It's Brandon's family's lake house. I've only been here a handful of times, but there is no mistaking this place. If the rooster theme didn't give it away, the family photos do.

He deposits my body next to the sofa. The man doesn't even bother to lift me onto the soft cushions, he just leaves me on the hard wooden floor. I look forward to the day that Karma bites him in the ass. When it does, I hope I get a front row seat.

Brandon goes about turning on lights and grabbing a bottle of water from the refrigerator. Meanwhile, I lay as still and limp as possible. If I can fool him into thinking I'm still affected by the sedative, then maybe I can buy myself some time to sneak out and run away. Where I'll run to, I have no idea. There aren't many houses out here. The ones that are here most likely won't be occupied this time of the year.

Setting his water on the end table near the recliner, Brandon squats down next to me and lifts my arm. I do my best to stay limp. When he lets my hand go, I let it fall to the floor with a thump. "Hum." He tests my other arm. "I didn't think that sedative would last this long."

Good. He believes I'm still drugged. My plan is working out beautifully. Hopefully, I'll be able to escape soon. I just need for him to leave the room long enough for me to sneak out the front door. Those brown eyes narrow as he studies me. Sweat starts to dot my forehead as I fear he may have seen right through my little act.

To my relief, he stands and heads down the hallway. Glancing back, he says, "Don't go running off." Laughter echoes in the empty space as he turns on his heel and enters the bathroom.

Counting to three, I quietly push myself from the floor. My limbs are still weak, but not useless, thank God. Since he kidnapped me from home, I'm barefoot, which works in my favor. It keeps my footsteps silent.

Standing is a bit of a chore. Dizziness overwhelms my senses once I'm upright, and I reach for the arm of the sofa to steady myself. I need to hurry if I want to get out of here before he returns. A look over my shoulder reveals that the bathroom door is still closed.

Using every ounce of strength I possess, I force my feet to move. One foot in front of the other until I'm standing at the front door. That little bit of movement is laborious and sweat dampens my hair, dripping into my eyes.

Jeez, at the rate I'm going, I'm not sure I'll get far before he exits the bathroom and realizes I'm gone. I can't take that risk. Turning the deadbolt, I open the front door and step outside. The sound of waves in the distance is like a lullaby. If I weren't trying to escape this hell, I would be tempted to lay on a lounger and let the sound carry me off to sleep.

On the third step down, I lose my footing and grab the railing to keep from tumbling down the remaining stairs. Once I get my bearings, I hurry down the last two and walk as fast as I can toward the trees. They will offer a small amount of cover, so I'm not as easily seen. Freedom is so close I can taste it.

The minute I reach the corner of the house, an arm snakes out, effectively clotheslining me. I fall backward, landing on my ass. Brandon's laughter is heard before his body appears from his hiding spot. "I had a feeling you were faking." Bending down, he lifts me up, throwing me over his shoulder like a sack of potatoes. "I figured I would climb out the bathroom window and wait for you to make your move."

Damnit, I should have known that little escape was too easy.

"Time to get you back inside." I kick, trying to throw him off balance and hopefully loosen his hold on me. His left arm tightens around my thighs and just as I lift my fists to pound on his back, I feel a pinch in my hip. Shit, that burns. "Yeah, I came prepared with your next dose. While you're out cold, I'll add some restraints."

TWENTY-SIX
Silas

Wesley and I sit at the kitchen table with Amy, who is currently tapping her fingernails on the tabletop. Normally I would be able to tune it out, but tonight her tapping is infuriating. It makes me want to rip her hair out and toss her ass outside.

Damn, not knowing what is happening to Monika has me feeling unstable as hell. I feel like I'm on the verge of a mental breakdown. Nothing has ever made me lose my shit like this. Only her. Lord, help me, if something happens to her. The world will feel my wrath and burn with my fury.

"So, I may have a lead." Wesley blows out a breath and levels his eyes on me. "It may be nothing, but my gut is telling me otherwise. Especially after finding out someone tampered with your security cameras."

Amy's tapping ceases as she leans forward to listen to what Wesley has to say. Her eyes are red rimmed from crying. A testament of her love for Monika.

Wesley sips his Coke then pinches the bridge of his nose. "A Millie Boone came into the station yesterday about a missing person."

What the hell does a young woman with a missing person's case have to do with Monika? I'm just about to voice this when my cousin continues.

He clasps his hands in front of him. "Her boyfriend, Brandon Miller, has not been seen in four weeks."

"Brandon Miller?" Is this the same Brandon from Monika's past? The douchebag that talked shit about her weight. Glancing over at my sister, I seek the answer to my unspoken question.

Amy nods in confirmation. "Monika's ex."

"What does his disappearance have to do with Monika?" But as the words leave my mouth, past incidences are brought back to remembrance. The car sitting in the empty parking lot of the clinic well after hours. A car Monika confirmed belonging to Brandon. The note left on her windshield. The accident.

The accident that happened four weeks ago. Shit.

"The accident?" I ask.

Amy sits ramrod straight. "You don't think he was responsible for that hit and run, do you?"

Wesley taps his thumb on the tabletop. His eyes slowly rising to meet mine. "I think it's a real possibility."

"But the car that hit her was reported as a silver SUV. Monika saw a silver car, not Brandon's." Amy presses her palms flat on the table. "Brandon drives a red Mazda."

Wesley takes this all in. "He could have gotten a new car, rented a car, or hell, he could have painted his car."

Time stops and my heart ceases along with it. What lengths will Brandon go to when it comes to Monika? Is he insane and desperate, or is this a ploy to win her back? No, he isn't trying to win her back. If that were the case, then that would mean he's in love with her. I know damn good and well that Brandon doesn't love Monika. Men in love don't verbally tear down their woman.

Speaking of, I have a sneaky suspicion that Brandon wasn't just verbally abusive. Monika has never hinted of anything physical, but there's little things that will cause her to shrink back. For instance, when Jose dropped a metal tray at the clinic, Monika ducked her head and shrugged her shoulders to her ears. Almost as if she was afraid a hand was about to connect with her face.

"The day of Monika's accident is the last time Millie saw Brandon. I would say there's a pretty good chance he is the culprit." Wesley turns his gaze to my sister. "Do you have any idea where he would have taken her?"

"No." She shakes her head, dark stands of hair whipping her face. "If he's not at home, I have no clue where he would be."

Wesley gives us a rundown of every place they've searched for Brandon, including his place of employment. Since he has not shown up for work in four weeks, the business has cut their losses and let him go. Knowing that he hasn't shown up for work since her accident sure as shit makes him look guilty.

The more my cousin talks, the bigger this hollowness in my chest grows. My stomach is in knots from agonizing worry. Worry that she's scared and hurt, and I'm not there to help. Worry that I will never see her again, and with that possibility hanging over my head, my heart breaks. Like physical pain splintering the beating organ in my chest. Each heartstring pulling taut, threatening to snap.

God, this hurts. It hurts worse than when I had my wisdom teeth pulled. Hurts worse than the time I sliced my arm with a box cutter, and I sliced it deep enough to require several stitches. Fisting my hand over my heart, I rub circles, trying to alleviate the pain.

Amid listening to Wesley, Amy jumps out of her chair. "The lake house." Arms flailing, she shouts, "Did you check the lake house?"

This gets my attention, bringing a sliver of hope to my soul. Wesley stops tapping his thumb on the tabletop, mouth still open midsentence and snapping shut. Shifting in his chair, he leans forward. "What lake house?"

If he didn't know about the lake house, then he hasn't looked there. That tidbit of information expands the hope currently infiltrating my weary heart. We may find her yet. *Oh God, help us find her. I will do anything if you just bring her back to me.*

"His parents own a house out on Okmulgee Lake." Amy swipes the screen of her cell phone. "He only took her a couple of times, I think." Swiftly, her finger scrolls through her phone until she finds what she's looking for. "Here's a picture, I'm not sure of the exact location."

Wesley takes the phone, scrutinizing the photo. His eyes moving from corner to corner. Wanting a look, I lean over and examine the photo on the screen. Wesley zooms in at the same time I point to the top right.

This particular area is one Wesley and I know well. Back in high school, we came here every weekend. The house in the distance is where we used to party. It was the quarterback's family lake house. "Holy shit," we say in unison.

Wesley lays Amy's cell phone on the table and dials the station. I slide the phone to my sister and point to the house in the background. "That's Jimmy's place."

My sister's eyes light up with hope. "So, you know where to find Brandon?"

I nod. "Yes."

Knowing where Brandon's lake house is, is one thing. Finding Monika is another. I hope and pray that this tiny bit of information leads us to her. Every second that she is missing gives him the opportunity to take her further from us. Or worse.

Amy stands and slings her purse over her shoulder. "What are you waiting for, let's go."

Wesley tucks his cell phone in his back pocket. "I called in back up." He holds up his keys. "I'll drive."

The entire drive, my leg bounces uncontrollably. It's a nervous tick I never knew I had. The last of the sun is setting and darkness is finally settling in. I worry about what we're about to walk in on. Too many late-night true crime shows are rising to remembrance, causing fear to wreak havoc on my mind.

When the pavement turns to rock, I snap my gaze to the windshield. His house is just half a mile up this road and to the left. The closer we get, the faster my heart beats. If I don't calm my heartrate, I'm afraid I'll start to feel faint. So, I focus on my breathing. It helps, but my nerves are countering my efforts.

As the car slows to a stop at the end of the street, I unbuckle my seatbelt. There are two cars sitting in the driveway and I sit up to get a better look. One of those cars appear to be a silver SUV. Holy hell, Brandon is the one that hit Monika.

I reach for the doorhandle and Wesley shakes his head. "You two are going to stay in the car. I have no idea what I'll be walking in on."

If I were an outsider looking in, I would wholeheartedly agree with my cousin. But I'm not an outsider, I'm right smack in the middle of it. This is personal and I'll be damned if I sit here and do nothing while Monika is in there suffering through God knows what. "No." Jerking my thumb behind me where my sister is sitting, I say, "She can stay, but I'm coming."

"Now wait just a damn minute." Amy unbuckles her seatbelt in one swift motion. "I am not sitting here while you macho men run into danger."

Wesley pinches the bridge of his nose. "You two give me a headache." Locking eyes with my sister, he says, "You stay, that's non-negotiable." When she starts to protest, he shakes his head. "I mean it, I'll take your ass back to town if I have to." Inhaling deeply, he releases it through his nose. "I would rather not waste another minute. So, please just stay put."

I guess he knows I'm not backing down. He motions toward my hip, where I keep my gun concealed. Knowing he's inquiring if I'm carrying, I confirm what he's silently asking. "Yes, I have my Glock with me." Living in the city all those years, though I wasn't in a high crime area, I did take a class and purchase a gun. It's habit for me to holster it to my hip when I'm not in the clinic.

"Good." Without another word, he opens his door and exits the vehicle.

Amy is already opening her door when I get out. "Don't make me cuff you to this car. If Brandon is armed, I don't want you getting in the crossfire. Besides, Monika needs you safe when we bring her out."

Since time is not on our side, I run after Wesley and pray that my sister obeys our instructions. I cannot afford to get sidetracked on this mission. We run along the shadows. The few houses on this street lack activity. All but one.

Brandon's.

We run through the neighbor's yard, moving from tree-to-tree to keep concealed. The bang of a door slamming shut draws my attention to the backyard. A man storms down the steps. "Damnit, Monika."

Thank God, we found her. By the looks of things, she is causing trouble for this asshole. Good. Now that we are here, we are going to rock his world, and not for the better. Standing in the middle of the yard, he searches the area. When he doesn't find what he's looking for, he circles around and heads toward the front.

He pauses for a moment, staring down the street where we parked the car. Shit. I hope he doesn't go investigating and find my sister. No telling what he would do to her. Maybe I should have let her come with us.

Instead of heading in the direction of the car, he starts searching the front yard. In addition to scanning the area and street, he kneels to look under both of the vehicles parked in his driveway. While he is pre-occupied, we tiptoe to the back of the house.

TWENTY-SEVEN
Monika

My head throbs like the waves of an angry ocean. Ugh, I feel as green as the wicked witch. Somebody please shoot me. Just put me out of my misery. This is the worst feeling in the world. I think I would rather have my teeth pulled with no anesthesia to block the pain.

That blasted nausea is back, worse than before. Of course, that could be a side effect from the sedative on an empty stomach. Bitterness coats the back of my throat and I lean over to spit out the bile. I roll partially when something tugs on my right hand, holding me in place. Once I empty my stomach of the vile acid, I take in the handcuffs.

Each wrist is cuffed to the wooden bedframe. I tug on the restraints, hoping for a little give, but they're locked on tightly. How the hell did Brandon come across these metal handcuffs? They look top notch. Makes me wonder if he has a kink, or if he's been planning this for some time.

I guess I never really knew that man.

Footsteps echo from the hallway and I close my eyes, hoping he doesn't realize I'm awake. The door creaks open and a shadow falls over me. I do my best to control my breathing, so I don't give myself away.

His presence is palpable, almost suffocating. I want to cry. Scream. Anything to release the tension building inside me. The moment is so intense. I wonder if this is what characters in horror movies feel when they're hiding from the killer.

Bang.

The sound of a metal tray hitting the headboard causes me to jump, ruining my efforts. Brandon laughs. "Liar, liar, pants on fire." I open my eyes to find him staring down at me, a syringe in one hand, a metal tray in the other. "You didn't think you could fool me twice, did you?"

That syringe frightens me. Mostly because I have no clue what is going on while I'm unconscious. Secondly, I have no chance of escaping if I'm out cold. "Please don't drug me. That stuff makes me nauseous."

Glancing down at the floor, he wrinkles his nose in disgust. "So, I see."

Tilting the syringe, he flicks a finger against the barrel. Afraid he is about to inject me yet again, I beg. "Please, Brandon." Tugging on the restraints, I say, "I'm already tied up, where am I going to go?"

This seems to give him pause. He eyes the cuffs for a moment. The whole time my heart is pounding loudly in my ears. "True." Waving the syringe in my face, he snarls. "But if you even thing about trying anything, I will jab you so fast, you won't know what hit you."

Digging up the girl I've spent so much time burying, I force tears to my eyes. This girl is afraid of everything that might anger Brandon. She is scared to disappoint him, knowing his wrath is never far away. It's not always physical lashings. No, it's psychological as well.

And the psychological lashings hurt worse than the physical ones.

Calling this part of me forth is something I must do to survive. If he believes that I'm still that terrified, self-conscious girl, then he will underestimate me. Leaving me with a sliver of a chance to get the hell out of dodge.

Setting the syringe on the dresser, he pulls a chair up beside the bed. "So, you thought you could leave me and play house with that dog doctor?"

We both know that I didn't leave him, it was the other way around. Though I'm not going to say that out loud. Instead, I sniffle and shrink into myself. Just like the old me would. "I'm sorry."

"You're right." Leaning back in the chair, he props his feet on the mattress. "You're a sorry piece of shit. Parading around with that fake-ass doctor, making a mockery of me." He kicks my thigh and then crosses his feet at the ankle. "Your behavior is downright embarrassing. Did you even stop to think what other people would think of me?"

What people would think of him? We are not together. Hadn't been for a while. How does my moving on make him look bad? Sometimes I wonder if he even knows what he's saying. I'm thinking his momma dropped him on the head one too many times.

Conjuring up all the sadness I can muster, I force myself to cry. Not just the few tears I managed a few minutes ago. No, I force big, fat tears to the surface. Letting them stream down my cheeks to soak the pillow beneath my head. "I'm so sorry."

This time he doesn't say anything. He just leans his head back, breathing deeply. If he's trying to control his breathing, then he is starting to lose the fire in his anger. It means that he is calming down and I may get to reason with him yet.

Not wanting to rush this, I stay silent and give him the quiet that he needs. I've been through this enough times, I know the routine. Slow and steady wins the race. Yes, I know this is a completely different situation, but the words still apply.

When his breathing settles, I decide to make my next move. Turning sorrowful eyes toward Brandon, I ask, "Can you forgive me?" I don't mean the words coming from my mouth. How can I. I'm not the one in the wrong. Yet, I will say whatever it takes to get me out of this situation.

"Hum." No words follow, and he doesn't even grace me with

a glance. That's okay, I don't need his attention. All I need is an opportunity to get out of here. Several minutes pass and Brandon finally sits up. "I'm going to shower." Looking down at my bound hands, he smirks. "Don't go running off."

Laughter fills the space around us as he gathers his clothes from the dresser. As soon as he exits the bedroom, I roll my eyes and mock him. Seconds later I can hear the water spray and I start looking around for keys, or anything I can use to pick the lock on these cuffs.

Have I ever picked a lock before? No. Is that going to stop me from trying? Again, no.

The nightstands on either side of the bed are both void of anything useful. Not that I could reach it with my hands, but since my feet are not bound, I figure I could twist my body until I could reach it with my feet and use my toes to grab it.

Brandon has never been one to take long showers, so I know my time is limited. Sweat dots my forehead as I glance around and find nothing to get these cuffs off with. This might be the only chance I get tonight since he is a very light sleeper.

Panic flares and my breathing escalates. I'm running out of time. When the shower shuts off, I know it's now or never. An idea flits through my mind. A memory from a television show that I've seen. If I can manage to break my thumbs, I should be able to wiggle my hands out of the handcuffs. Damn, this is going to hurt. Let's hope I can keep quiet, or else Brandon will come and sedate me again.

Turning my head, I scrutinize the headboard. My hands are bound too far apart for me to touch them together. Shit, how am I supposed to break my thumb if I can't reach it? Think, think, think.

Then it dawns on me. I'll have to use the headboard. Adjusting my hand just right, I press the back of my thumb against the wood. Pain shoots into my wrist, zinging up to the elbow. Oh God, how am I going to do this?

When he starts whistling, I know I must work fast. Inhaling

deeply, I hold my breath and press my thumb into the wood as hard as I can. *Crack.* The explosion of pain is like none other I've experienced, and I still have to slip my hand free and work on the other.

Metal bites into my flesh as I wiggle my hand free. Blood trickles from the cuts, but I manage to get my hand loose. Now to focus on the other before he returns. Using my ring and pinky fingers, I grip the edge of the pillow and bring it to my mouth, so I have something to bite into.

Breaking this thumb doesn't hurt as much as the first. Maybe it's because adrenaline has kicked in and my senses are dulling. It doesn't matter why it hurts less. All that matters is that I'm free and Brandon is still in the bathroom.

Rolling off the bed, I'm happy to discover that the sedative has fully worn off and I'm no longer dizzy and disoriented. Peeking around the door, I glance down the hall toward the bathroom. I can't risk tiptoeing to the front door, he may see me as I pass by.

Looks like I'll be going out the window. Using my middle and index fingers, I slide the lock over. My heart is pounding so loud I fear I won't hear him when he comes back into the room. Glancing over my shoulder, I see that I'm still alone. Good. Hurrying, I use those same fingers to raise the window. It takes longer than I like to remove the screen, but I get it off just in time.

Footsteps in the hallway has me moving faster. I slip my legs over the windowsill and jump to the ground. There is no way I am risking being seen by shutting the window, so I take off running as fast as my legs will carry me.

On the backside of the property are several trees. I dash in that direction and sprint for cover. This lake house community is empty, no lights on in any of the other houses. Meaning I have no one I can run to for help.

"Damnit, Monika," Brandon shouts and I fall to the ground, army crawling behind a small log that I'm sure isn't big enough to conceal my frame, but it's all I've got.

I peek around the edge and see him standing in the backyard scanning the area. Holding my breath, I lay as still as possible. His body is facing my direction and I'm afraid he knows exactly where I am.

Just when I think he's going to come for me, he turns and heads in the other direction. Thank God. I exhale and start to stand when I see a figure in the shadows. Oh God, what now? One danger is bad enough, I'm not sure I can handle two. Especially with two broken thumbs.

TWENTY-EIGHT
Silas

The house is quiet, which I expect since Brandon left the house shouting for Monika. While he's outside, I want to make sure she isn't inside hiding from him. Wesley searches the kitchen and living room while I head for the bathroom and bedrooms.

Pushing open the first door I come to, I use my cell phone's flashlight and scan the area. Including the closet and under the bed. There is nothing here except some dust on the dresser. Exiting the room, I head for the bathroom. The door is wide open, and steam is still thick in the air.

A quick look inside and I know she's not in there. There is one more room and the door is open with the light on. I whisper, "Monika?" Nothing. As I fully enter the room, I see the handcuffs dangling from the headboard.

Anger boils in my blood and my nostrils flare as I breathe. I swear to all that is holy, if he harmed one hair on her head, I will lose my shit. I'm not above doing some jail time for exacting revenge. Not only will he suffer, but he'll be lucky if I let him survive. You don't mess with a man's family and walk away unscathed.

Approaching the bed, I take stock of the cuffs. Red smears on both handcuffs is enough to seal that asshole's fate. Footsteps slap the hardwood floors behind me, and I turn around, gun aimed and ready.

Wesley stops in his tracks. "It's me." I lower the gun. "Did you find anything?"

Motioning toward the headboard, I nod. "Sure did, and that bastard is going to pay."

A blood curdling scream raises the hairs on my arms. Wesley and I both sprint back the way we came. He is the first to burst through the back door. I'm hot on his heels. At first, I don't see anything. Turning, I start for the front but stop when Monika screams again. "Let me go, you psycho."

Running blind, I head for the trees that line the back perimeter of the property. My cousin's footsteps match mine as we search for Monika. In the distance, I can hear the sound of vehicles. I sure hope that is the backup that Wesley called in earlier. Why the hell did it take them this long to get here?

Movement to my right draws my attention. I point as I veer in that direction. Wesley's footsteps fall in line with mine. As we get closer, we slow our steps and move from tree-to-tree for cover.

Pain filled sobs echo in the night, and it takes everything inside me not to dash to Monika's rescue. Wesley holds up a hand, silently telling me to stay put. Since he's the professional, I'll let him lead this shindig.

"I told you if you tried to escape again, I would jab you." Brandon has Monika pinned to the ground, holding her hands above her head. Her legs kick wildly, but he's straddling her, and her kicks are to no avail.

The urge to shoot is strong, but with how close he is lying on her, and the way they are wrestling for control, I'm afraid of hitting her instead. Wesley takes slow and steady steps toward them.

Brandon is so focused on Monika that he seems to be oblivious to our arrival. That is, until I shift my foot and step on a twig. The crack is loud enough he lifts his head and glances in my direction.

You mean to tell me that our frantic running didn't catch his attention, but this tiny little twig did? Just my luck. "Whose out there?" he shouts.

It doesn't appear that he has noticed my cousin, so I go ahead and step out of the shadows and trust that Wesley can handle the situation. The gun in my right hand is hidden behind my back.

"Who the hell are you?" The grip on Monika doesn't lessen, but her head turns to get a look.

The instant she sees me, her body relaxes in his hold. Not because she trusts the man holding her captive, but because she trusts me to get her out of this situation safely. "Let's talk this through."

The laughter that comes out of Brandon is sinister. Obviously, he has lost all sanity. Which is scary, because that means that he will go to any lengths to get what he wants. Including ending her life if he feels it's the only way. So, I need to play this as cautiously as possible.

"Silas?" Monika's voice wobbles with fear, but I sense pain in there as well. Which reminds me of the bloody handcuffs.

God, I have never wanted to kill anyone as much as I want to kill him. But I can't afford to lash out now. Not while he has her in his clutches.

At the sound of my name on her lips, he secures both her wrists in one hand then rears back and slaps her across the face. My body is shaking with anger now. Taking a deep breath, I try reasoning with the asshole. "Hey, over here." At the sound of my voice, Brandon seems to remember that I'm still here and turns a glare in my direction. "You need to release her. The cops will be here any minute and you don't want to spend time in jail for kidnapping and assaulting her."

He gazes around like he's looking for those cops that I mentioned. Taking advantage of his distraction, I inch forward. Sensing my nearness, he jumps to his feet, dragging Monika up with him. "Stay back or I swear I'll break her neck."

Moonlight hits her face and I see the tear streaks on her cheeks and the fear in her eyes. In my peripheral, I see Wesley moving.

Brandon must see him too because he reaches behind his back and pulls out a gun. Cold fear swims down my spine.

Wesley steps out from the shadows. "Put the gun down."

"You two think you're going to take me down?" Lifting the gun, he plants the nozzle to Monika's temple. "You'll have to go through her first."

Shit. Having a gun against her temple paralyzes me. It's like my brain has forgotten how to send signals to the rest of my body. I'm nothing but an empty vessel, completely useless as I watch the horror playing out in front of me.

"You don't want to do that." Wesley keeps his gun trained on Brandon and I pray he doesn't do anything to get her killed. "Murder will land you straight in prison."

"None of this would have happened if he," Brandon jerks his head toward me, "had just kept his hands to himself."

He's blaming me for his insanity?

If you had told me months ago that my life would end up like this, I would have told you that you were crazy. That this sounds like a dramatic episode of a LifeTime thriller. How is this real life.

"I swear to God, if you don't drop that gun, I'm going to blow her brains out," Brandon screams. I have no doubt that he's serious. His gaze cuts to me. "You too. Don't think I haven't noticed your hand behind your back."

Keeping Monika safe is my number one priority, so I toss the gun to the side and raise both hands. "I'm unarmed, just let her go. Let's settle this between us like men."

"Hell no." His hold on her tightens. "I'm not stupid. The minute I release her, this idiot over here is going to shoot me."

"No." Wesley moves a fraction closer. "If you release her, we can let this go."

"You think I don't watch those cop shows?" Brandon shakes his head. "No, you'll cuff me and lock me away."

"Come on, do the right thing." Wesley takes another step toward them.

Where my cousin looks cool, calm, and collected, I'm a total mess. My nerves are shot all to hell, and my heart is pounding so hard I may pass out. I realize how dumb that sounds. I'm a man, I should be made of steel. In any other circumstance I would be, but this is Monika, and seeing her in this dire situation is killing me.

Seeing my cousin closing in, Brandon panics and I see his finger twitch on the trigger. "If I can't have her, no one can."

Bang.

My heart drops to the pit of my stomach and a scream burst out of me. One so loud I'm sure everyone in Okmulgee County hears.

TWENTY-NINE
Monika

Bang.

The first gunshot is followed by two more. Ringing in my ears is slightly disorienting. I'm not sure what is going on, but Silas is screaming and running toward me. His eyes wide and tortured.

Wesley is shouting and running as well. Meanwhile, heaviness pushes me downward. My body hits the ground with a thud, sending pain jolting through my hip and chin. It becomes burdensome to suck in air.

My body hurts everywhere, and I just want to go home. Wesley and Silas reach me at the same time. When Silas crouches down beside me, I see tears pool in his gray eyes. I'm not sure why he's crying.

Footsteps pound the ground behind me. Oh God, is it Brandon? Is he coming to finish what he started?

Wetness coats my neck, dripping onto the ground under me. I try to lift my hand to the source, but it feels as though there is a weight pinning it down. Wesley squats next to Silas, his concerned gaze examining my face. "You're okay, we're going to get you out of here." His eyes lift, then lower back down to mine. "My friend Jason is here to help. Don't be alarmed when you feel him behind you."

Silas traces a finger down my cheek, his eyes have not left me for a single second. "You're okay, sweetheart. I'm here. I've got you."

I think all the excitement from this ordeal, combined with the pain from my broken thumbs, is starting to get to me. My eyelids are getting heavy, and a chill envelops my body, causing me to shiver.

Warm hands touch my back. The warmth doing nothing to heat my skin where they touch. I'm so cold that I'm numb. Closing my eyes, I lay still, reveling in the feel of Silas's touch. I could use a week's worth of sleep. Or more.

Those hands that are touching my back tug and suddenly a weight lifts and I can breathe freely. A sigh blows past my lips and then I'm being hauled into Silas's lap. His fingers run through my hair as he rocks us back and forth.

Now that I'm not lying face down on the ground, I see what was pulled off my back. Brandon is sprawled out on the ground, motionless. The next thing I see has bile rising up the back of my throat. Three holes in his head are spilling blood onto the ground. Blood that I just now realize is coating my neck.

They shot him while he was holding me captive. His body is the heaviness on me that made it hard to draw breath. In one sense, I feel horrible. In the profession I'm in, life is precious. We do what we can to save lives, albeit animals, but lives nonetheless. However, I'm very thankful that I am alive and well, and Brandon will never harm me again.

I will no longer suffer at the hands of my ex, and that is all that matters.

Silas picks up one of my hands, inspecting my wrist. He traces the angry red lines from where the handcuffs bit into my skin. Then he jerks my hand closer to his face. "What the hell, Monika?"

Glancing at my hand, I see that my thumb is swollen and purplish. Lifting my other hand, I see it looks just as bad. Silas sucks in air when he takes stock of both hands. Wesley, who has been talking with his men, now comes over. He grimaces when he sees the state that I'm in. "Damn, broke your thumbs to escape, huh?"

I nod. "I had to. I couldn't risk another minute in that house."

"Smart thinking," Wesley says. "You did good."

Sirens blare in the distance. Silas stands with me in his arms. "Come on, sweetheart. Let's get you to the hospital." He carries me to the driveway, where he lays me on a stretcher being pushed by paramedics.

"Monika." The sound of Amy's voice is music to my ears. "Oh my God, I was so scared." She grips my hand to comfort me. White hot pain shoots through my hand and I scream. Instantly, she releases me. When she notices my swollen and bruised thumbs, she tears up. "I'm so sorry."

When the paramedics get me loaded into the ambulance, Silas hops in. The paramedic holds his hand out to stop Amy from entering. "Sorry, only one passenger is allowed."

Amy ducks under his arm. "You'll have to make an exception. I'm not going anywhere." Then she climbs into the rig, taking a seat next to her brother.

The last eight weeks have been ridiculously boring. Again, I'm stuck at home with nothing to do but watch television. Silas's orders, of course. He goes to work every day, but he has had Doctor Allen there to help out since I'm out of commission. That, and Silas feels the need to come check on me periodically during the day.

Amy has been just as protective of me lately. If she's off work, she's here. On her lunch break, she's here. Between the two of them, I feel overwhelmed. I was kidnapped and injured, it's not like the trauma has left me incapacitated. I can still take care of myself. Some tasks have been more challenging than others, but I manage.

One thing I am appreciative of is the added security cameras.

Brandon may no longer grace this earth, but he isn't the only psychopath out there. Our new security alerts us when our perimeters have been breached. Not only do we get the notification on our phones, a red light flashes in each room, followed by a series of beeps. Which I am very thankful for.

Today was my follow up visit with my doctor. Both thumbs have healed nicely, and I have been cleared to go back to work, on light duty. Silas has been trying to convince me take an extra couple of weeks off, but there is no way I can sit at home any longer. I'll go batshit crazy if I have to stay home another day. I'm ready to get back to caring for all the fur babies that come into our facility.

Speaking of those flashing red lights, the corner of the living room lights up to alert me of a visitor. I immediately hop up from the sofa and peer out the window. A silver Camry cruises up the drive and I smile. As much as her hovering annoys me, it's still good to see her. A friend like her is a rare find, and I cherish our friendship. Even if she is overbearing lately.

Opening the front door, I meet her on the porch. "Hey." She reaches into the backseat, and I wonder what she's got this time. When she shuts the car door, I see a large white box in her hand. "What do you have?"

Ascending the porch steps, she grins and gives me a side hug. "Something for you to try on." What on earth did she go out and do? "Here." Passing the box to me, she waves for me to enter the house.

Amy follows me to the bedroom. When I pry the lid off the box, I see a burgundy dress. "Whoa, what is this for?" It's not just any dress, this is a sexy cocktail dress.

"Just put it on already." In her hand is a bag. A shoe bag. Chances are, they're shoes to go with the dress.

When I slip the dress on, I turn so she can zip me up. Staring at myself in the mirror, I can't believe what I see. The dress fits like it was tailored just for me. "It's beautiful."

"No." Amy smiles. "You're beautiful." Handing over the shoe

bag, she adds, "Now put these on. I picked them out myself." Inside the are a pair of silver heels. They pair with the dress perfectly. As I knew they would. This is Amy we're talking about. She has impeccable taste.

Amy helps with my hair and makeup, wanting me to look perfect. Why, I have no idea. It's not like I plan on going anywhere tonight. Silas and I have agreed to eat takeout and watch a movie. In fact, he should be home any minute now.

"There, you're absolutely glowing." Amy steps back to get a good look at her handiwork.

"Yes," I agree. "But this is a bit overkill for takeout and movie night."

"Oh, baby girl." Amy chuckles. "You aren't having takeout and watching a movie." Tugging my arm, she leads me to the front door. "We're going out tonight."

"I can't." As much as I'd love to have a date night with my best friend, I refuse to bail on Silas. Not when we have solid plans. Luca jumps off the back of the sofa and rubs against my legs. "See, even Luca knows I can't go out tonight."

"Don't be absurd." Amy picks up my tiny ball of fur, placing him back on the sofa. "Besides, I already cleared it with Silas."

I'm shocked that she butted into my relationship like that. "You did?"

"Yep, and he's going out with Wesley."

What the hell, he made plans of his own without telling me? We never cancel on one another. Ever. Guess there's a first time for everything. I let Amy lead me out to her car. "Where are we going?"

Buckling her seatbelt, she throws a grin my way. "The Lodge."

Oh boy, they must be having a party tonight. Amy is always up for music, dancing, and drinking. I gaze out the window during the fourteen-minute drive. The whole time I'm wishing that Silas was with me.

I wonder why he made plans and told his sister but not me.

Inside, the place is not as hopping as I thought it would be.

Especially for a Friday night. Amy takes the lead, heading toward the back where the banquet room is. The lack of activity in this place is quit unnerving.

Stepping inside the banquet hall, I gasp in surprise. Balloons fill the room, along with all our friends. Including Silas's parents, and stepparents. "What is going on?" I ask Amy.

Flashing me her pearly whites, she says, "Come on in and find out." Leaving me to stand at the entrance, Amy skips over to her mother. The two embrace and then glance my way. Feeling like an oddball, I step further into the room. Unsure what is happening right now.

The crowd parts like the red sea, and Silas emerges, carrying a bouquet of red roses. I'm not sure what this man is up to, but I walk toward him, meeting him in the middle. "Hey, sweetheart."

"Hey." I twist my hands together, unsure of what this is. It's not our anniversary or my birthday. We already had a belated celebration for my missed party. Silas offers the roses to me. The first thing I do is smell them. I don't know what it is about fresh flowers, but they soothe me. "They're beautiful."

His lips turn up in a sexy smile. "So are you." Those gray pools trail up and down my body, sending shivers down my spine. "In fact, I think I'll have you for dessert tonight." Licking his lips, he adds, "You look downright delectable in that dress."

Embarrassment heats my cheeks at those words, and I glance around to see if anyone has overheard. My insides relax when it appears no one has heard what Silas said to me. I don't know what I'm going to do with this man. "Stop," I whisper shout. "Your parents are here. What if they had overheard you talk to me like that."

"Sweetheart." Silas kisses my nose. "We're both adults. What I say to you is none of their concern." He lifts his hand in the air, giving a signal. A signal for what, I haven't a clue. But then music pours from the speakers. *Marry You* by Bruno Mars.

To my surprise, Silas produces a microphone from seemingly out of nowhere. As he sings the words to the song, everyone in the room watches, but I pay them no attention. Silas is my only focus right now as he holds my hand, singing a song about marriage.

Dare I believe he is about to do what I have dreamed of since childhood? I don't have to question his actions much longer, because as the song ends, he kneels and pulls a small black box from his pocket. "So, what do you say, sweetheart. Will you marry me?"

Dashing away a stray tear, I nod and fall to my knees. "Yes."

"Yeah?"

Everyone in this room fades away and it's only us. I wrap my arms around his neck, careful not to crush my roses, and kiss him. My childhood dream has now become my reality. The one thing I thought I would never have, is now all mine. With my lips still pressed to his, I say, "All the yeses. You have all of me."

A big smile lights up his face and he pulls away from the kiss. "I love you." Those three words melt my heart. Taking the ring from the box, he slips it on my finger. It twinkles in the low lighting, and I can't help but stare at my hand. Silas tugs me to my feet. "She said yes," he shouts.

As if they didn't already know. My actions were pretty obvious. Our friends and family cheer and whistle. Champagne is passed around, and people litter the dance floor. After Amy takes the roses from me, Silas and I join them, swaying to the slow music.

Our engagement party lasts well into the night. By the time we leave, I'm bordering drunk and ready to strip out of this dress. Silas has a possessive grip on my thigh as we drive home. The alcohol in my system has me horny as hell. Or maybe it's the fact it's been weeks since we have had sex. Don't get me wrong, Silas has definitely taken care of my needs, just not in the way I'd like.

Hiking my skirt up, I let my thighs fall open. "Monika, what are you doing?"

"Baby, it's been so long." Even to my own ears, my voice sound whiny. "I need you in the worst way." I do. My body feels like it will combust if I don't have him right this second.

"Is that so?"

"Yes." I scoot down in the seat, hinting that I need him to touch me. "Please."

His hand tightens on my thigh before it inches up my flesh, sliding beneath my lace panties. Yes, that's what I need. What I've been craving all night. "Damn, Monika, you're soaked." Using my juices, he rubs circles around my clit, setting my body on fire. "Have you needed me this badly all night?" Riding the waves of euphoria, I nod. It's all I can do as I lose myself to this man's touch. His finger stills and I groan in frustration, lifting my pelvis to get the friction I crave. Removing his finger from my flesh, he says, "Uh, uh. Use your words."

"Huh?" What words? I don't remember what he asked me. My mind is total mush.

"Answer me." Using the same hand that was in my panties, he grips my chin, turning my face toward him. "Have you needed me this badly all night?"

"Yes." It's the truth. I've been thinking about sex with Silas all day. My body needs more than just foreplay and one-sided orgasms. When I say one-sided, I mean him pleasing me but not wanting pleasure in return.

"Next time you tell me when you're desperate for my touch." Pulling into the driveway, he shuts off the engine and rushes to open the passenger side door. "Come on, sweetheart. Let's give your body what it needs."

Lifting me bridal style, he marches up the porch steps and fumbles with the keys. Holding my palm out, I take the keys from him and unlock the front door. Taking me to our bedroom, he lowers me to my feet beside the bed. Leaning forward, he kisses me tenderly. His fingers unzipping the dress in the process.

When the material pools at my feet, he is quick to lift me to the bed, tugging my panties down once I'm situated. Since the dress was strapless, I'm without a bra. He removes his suit jacket, folding it and laying it on the bedside table. With slow movements he undresses, his eyes never leaving mine.

If he doesn't hurry up, I may die right here. I'm so hot and on edge, I can feel the beginnings of flutters in my core. Once he is standing before me naked, he reaches for the drawer that holds the condoms.

Reaching out a hand, I say, "Not tonight. I want to feel all of you."

His eyes scan mine, searching for the truth. "You sure?"

Licking my lips, I nod. "Yes, one hundred percent sure."

Forgoing the condom, he climbs into bed, caressing my body with the pads of his fingers. Warm wet lips close over my hardened nipples and I arch into him, needing more. So much more.

One hand slithers down and rubs my tender flesh while his mouth sucks and nips my rock hard peaks. Jolts shoot through me. My thighs tightening around him as he rubs me through my orgasm. When the shockwaves fade, he moves up my body, aligning himself with my core.

As it always has been, pleasure rocks through me when he enters me. I moan, and hiss in a breath through my teeth. Our bodies were made for this. For one another. His hips pump faster and faster, and his kisses become sloppy. "Come on, sweetheart. Be my good girl and come one more time."

That's all it takes for my body to respond. I detonate and his hips move harder and faster, seeking his own release. With a final thrust, he grips my hip in one hand, squeezing. His body shakes with the release, stilling on mine as he rides the high.

Peppering my face with kisses, he says, "I love you, soon-to-be Mrs. McKade."

This night could not be more perfect. We had many hurdles to overcome, but we persevered. We have our clinic, each other, and our perfect little fluffy kitten with half a tail. What more could a girl want.

Meet Luca

Luca is my sweet boy who was rescued by my sister-in-law. He did lose half his tail after his mom and siblings left him behind. After being doctored up, we took him in. He grunts when he talks, and his meows come out as mer-ow-er. He loves lounging on the bed, soaking up the sun coming in through the window. And he is a momma's boy.

ABOUT Tich Brewster

Tich is a born and raised Oklahoma resident and the mother of six. Her passion for reading started at an early age when her Aunt Vicky gave her the novel Heidi for Christmas. She didn't start writing until middle school, after being inspired by her best friend's short stories.

Being a mom of six is a huge blessing and she is extremely grateful to be able to stay home with the children. Other than books, she loves coffee and candles. There is nothing more relaxing than drinking coffee and reading a book while the aroma of a fruity candle fills the air.

Join the reader group on Facebook: Tich's Book Haven
You can also sign up for her newsletter via her website

Connect with Tich Online

Facebook: @TichBrewsterAuthor
Instagram, X, TikTok: @TichBrewster